BASICS
FASHION DESIGN
03

Anette Fischer

CONSTRUCTION

Ethical: aware-
ness/
reflect-
ion/
debate

ava
academia

An AVA Book
Published by AVA Publishing SA
Rue des Fontenailles 16
Case Postale
1000 Lausanne 6
Switzerland
Tel: +41 786 005 109
Email: enquiries@avabooks.ch

Distributed by Thames & Hudson (ex-North America)
181a High Holborn
London WC1V 7QX
United Kingdom
Tel: +44 20 7845 5000
Fax: +44 20 7845 5055
Email: sales@thameshudson.co.uk
www.thamesandhudson.com

Distributed in the USA & Canada by:
Ingram Publisher Services Inc.
1 Ingram Blvd.
La Vergne, TN 37086
USA
Tel: +1 866 400 5351
Fax: +1 800 838 1149
Email: customer.service@ingrampublisherservices.com

English Language Support Office
AVA Publishing (UK) Ltd.
Tel: +44 1903 204 455
Email: enquiries@avabooks.ch

ISBN 978-2-940373-75-8

10 9 8 7 6 5 4 3

Design by Sifer Design

Production by AVA Book Production Pte. Ltd., Singapore
Tel: +65 6334 8173
Fax: +65 6259 9830
Email: production@avabooks.com.sg

1   Alexander McQueen, S/S09.
     Catwalking.com.

Contents

Construction

1   Sleeveless dress designed
     by David Bradley.

*'Do not quench your inspiration and your imagination;
do not become the slave of your model.'*

Vincent Van Gogh

Construction is the foundation of clothing and of fashion design;
it is vital that fashion designers know and understand the
techniques involved in creating a three-dimensional garment
from a two-dimensional design or pattern in order to create a
beautiful shape and fit on a moving body. Garment construction
involves both technical and design issues; the designer can
choose where to construct lines, pockets, collars, how to
finish edges and how to produce volume and structure in
order to create a unique look and experience for the wearer.

From basic block cutting to the smallest finishing
details on a constructed garment, *Basics Fashion Design:
Construction* leads you through the essential stages of
garment construction and offers you a starting point from
which knowledge can be extended. It introduces you to the
world of pattern cutting, draping on the mannequin and
shows you some techniques for breathing life into a flat
design drawing in order to achieve a three-dimensional
garment. Basic sewing techniques are introduced and you
are shown how to use darts, sleeves, collars, pockets and
the cut of the fabric to add variation to your designs. The
breadth of the subject is illustrated with a history of garment
construction, techniques used in the haute couture and tailoring
crafts and an introduction to supporting and structuring
materials. The book concludes with finishing techniques
and a selection of resources for those wishing to delve
deeper into the world of construction for fashion.

With its inspirational photography and easy-to-follow
diagrams, *Construction* offers a clear introduction to the
fundamental skills, knowledge and historical background
needed for successful garment construction. I hope it will
awaken your interest and inspire you to create the perfect
silhouette and a beautiful, final piece.

1

How to get the most out of this book

This book introduces different aspects of garment construction via dedicated chapters for each topic. Each chapter provides numerous examples of work by leading designers, annotated to explain the reasons behind the choices made.

Key construction and design principles are isolated so that the reader can see how they are applied in practice.

Clear navigation
Each chapter has a clear heading to allow readers to quickly locate areas of interest.

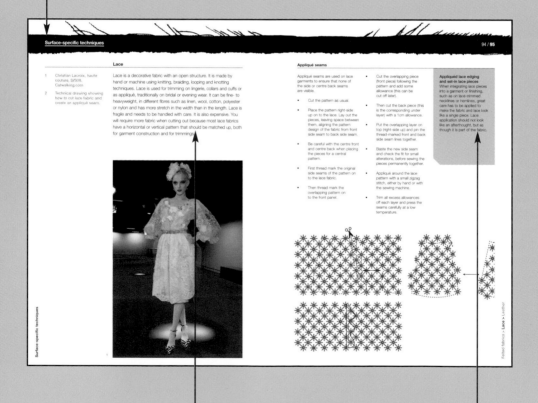

Lace

1   Christian Lacroix, haute
    couture, S/S06.
    Catwalking.com

2   Technical drawing showing
    how to cut lace fabric and
    create an appliqué seam.

Lace is a decorative fabric with an open structure. It is made by hand or machine using knitting, braiding, looping and knotting techniques. Lace is used for trimming on lingerie, collars and cuffs or as appliqué, traditionally on bridal or evening wear. It can be fine- to heavyweight, in different fibres such as linen, wool, cotton, polyester or nylon and has more stretch in the width than in the length. Lace is fragile and needs to be handled with care. It is also expensive. You will require more fabric when cutting out because most lace fabrics have a horizontal or vertical pattern that should be matched up, both for garment construction and for trimmings.

Appliqué seams

Appliqué seams are used on lace garments to ensure that none of the side or centre back seams are visible.

• Cut the pattern as usual.

• Place the pattern right-side up on to the lace. Lay out the pieces, leaving space between them, aligning the pattern design of the fabric from front side seam to back side seam.

• Be careful with the centre front and centre back when placing the pieces for a central pattern.

• First thread mark the original side seams of the pattern on to the lace fabric.

• Then thread mark the overlapping pattern on to the front panel.

• Cut the overlapping piece (front piece) following the pattern and add some allowance (this can be cut off later).

• Then cut the back piece (this is the corresponding under layer) with a 1cm allowance.

• Put the overlapping layer on top (right-side up) and pin the thread-marked front and back side seam lines together.

• Baste the new side seam and check the fit for small alterations, before sewing the pieces permanently together.

• Appliqué around the lace pattern with a small zigzag stitch, either by hand or with the sewing machine.

• Trim all excess allowances off each layer and press the seams carefully at a low temperature.

Appliquéd lace edging and set-in lace pieces
When integrating lace pieces into a garment or finishing, such as on lace-trimmed necklines or hemlines, great care has to be applied to make the fabric and lace look like a single piece. Lace application should not look like an afterthought, but as though it is part of the fabric.

Surface-specific techniques

Felted fabrics > **Lace** > Leather

Introductions
Special section introductions outline basic concepts that will be discussed.

Additional information
Box-outs elaborate on subjects discussed in the main text.

Captions
These provide image details and commentary to guide the reader in the exploration of the visuals displayed.

Headings
These enable the reader to break down text and refer quickly to topics of interest.

Examples
Imagery accompanying the rich content, visually describes elements such as seams, fabric, equipment etc.

Haute couture and tailoring

Tailoring techniques

1 An inside-out tailored jacket showing the under structure.

2 Woollen fabric and lining sample booklet, published by 2000 Tailoring Ltd, London.

3 Tailored jacket with basting stitching in working progress.

A lot of components play a significant role in creating an excellently fitted tailored garment, from the right choice of fabric and the shape and design of the garments, to the skilled measuring of the body and the specific techniques employed.

This section will introduce you to some of the materials and techniques used by tailors for constructing jackets.

The hand stitches

The following stitches are commonly used in tailoring:

Basting stitch attaches two or more pieces of fabric temporarily. It is also used to make construction and placement lines.

Pad stitching is used to attach the sew-in interfacing and to shape the garment at the same time.

Slip-stitch attaches the lining edge to the hem invisibly as well as the edges of pockets to the garment.

Fell stitching holds the stay tape in narrow fabric tape) in place.

Cross-stitch invisibly secures interfacing edges to the garment.

Hemstitching invisibly attaches the hem allowance to the garment.

Tailor's tacks are used to mark fabrics, for example on the folding line of the lapel rolling line or pocket placement.

Trimming, notching and grading

All edges in a tailored garment should be flat and sharp without noticeable bulk. Seam edges, collar tips and pocket flaps should roll slightly to the inside, towards the body. To avoid bulky seams use the following methods:

Trimming. Trim sewn-in interfacings close to the seam lines. The seam allowance of the collar, lapel and bagged-out pocket points can also be trimmed.

Notching. Notch the seam allowance by taking out wedges at the outside curves. On a deep curve bring notches closer together than on a shallow one. Always notch close to the stitching line.

Grading. Trim the seam allowance back in a staggered fashion whereby the widest seam allowance is layered towards the garment's right side. This is done to cushion the remaining seams, so they do not show through to the right side.

The understructure

This is made from different kinds of canvas and interfacing, soft cotton flannel, cotton twill tape, strips of cotton or lambswool, Melton for the collar stand, pocketing fabric and strong, lightweight lining.

The fabrics

Woollen fabric used for tailored suits can fall into two categories: worsteds and woollens. Worsted fabric is woven from long, finely combed wool. It is a firm fabric with a flat surface, ideal for traditional tailored business suits. Woollen fabrics are woven from shorter, uncombed wool fibres. These fibres are loosely twisted and woven much less tightly than the worsteds. The effect is a soft, easy fabric, such as a Harris Tweed. Other fabrics can also be used, such as silk and linen.

Tweed
A woollen fabric named after the river Tweed, which flows through the Scottish Borders textile areas. Harris Tweed is one variation, made from pure virgin wool that is dyed and spun in Harris (in the Outer Hebrides) and hand woven by the islanders in their homes.

The pressing techniques

Darts and seams create shape in a piece of fabric. It is best, therefore, to use a tailor's ham or a rounded pressing board to maintain the shape. Press the vertical darts upwards (centre front or centre back). If using a thick fabric, cut open the dart and press flat. To get a nice, flat point at the dart end use a needle and insert right to the point. Press with the needle in place and remove it afterwards.

Moulding is the stretching and shrinking of fabric to fit the body shape. The best fabric to use is wool, which takes on the new shape and holds it as if it had always been

To avoid over pressing, which causes the imprint of seams, edges and darts to appear on the outside, use paper strips or pieces of the same kind of fabric to underlay the seam allowance and edges.

that way. A tailor would reshape the two-piece sleeve to accentuate the forward bend in the elbow area. The trouser leg would be reshaped before a seam allowance in attached. For example, the back panel on the inside leg is stretched at the top to fit on to the front panel, thus achieving a closer fit to the bottom and crotch area.

Chapter titles
These run along the bottom of every page to provide clear navigation and allow the reader to understand the context of the information on the page.

Running footers
Clear navigation allows the reader to know where they are, where they have come from and where they are going in the book.

How to get the most out of this book

1   Jean Paul Gaultier, A/W07.
     Catwalking.com.

> *'Fashion is architecture. It is a matter of proportions.'*
>
> Coco Chanel

It is important for designers to understand as early as possible how a garment grows from a two-dimensional concept into a three-dimensional object. A pattern is a flat paper or card template, from which the parts of the garment are transferred to fabric, before being cut out and assembled.

A good understanding of body shape and how body measurements transfer to the pattern piece is essential. The pattern cutter must work accurately in order to ensure that, once constructed, the parts of fabric fit together properly and precisely.

This chapter is an introduction to pattern cutting, starting with the tools and equipment needed. Then it takes a look at the processes involved: the importance of silhouettes and proportion; sizing and grading and how to take body measurements. Finally it introduces the basic block and pattern shapes and how the body measurements relate to these.

Pattern cutting tools and equipment

Working with the right tools will make block and pattern construction easier. These are just some of the key pieces of equipment required.

Tailor's chalk (1)
Using tailor's chalk is one way of marking lines or transferring a pattern on to cloth.

Set of three French curves (2)
These are used for drawing narrower curves, such as those found on collars and pockets.

43cm set square (3)
This is a right-angled triangular plate used for drawing lines, particularly at 90 degrees and 45 degrees.

Wooden awl (4)
This is used for marking any points within the pattern piece by punching through the pattern to leave a small mark on the fabric.

Pins (5)
These are used to temporarily fix pieces of paper or cloth together.

Tape measure (6)
An indispensable item, this is used for taking measurements of the body and its flexibility allows curved lines to be measured too.

Pattern drill (7)
This is used for marking things such as darts, pockets and any other marking points within the pattern piece. The pattern drill will punch a hole of 2–4mm into the pattern. The position of the punch hole can then be marked with chalk or thread on to the fabric.

Pattern notcher (8)

This is used for marking the edge of the pattern pieces by taking out a small square for each balance point. This should only be used on pattern paper – thin sheets of plastic or card – not on fabric.

Paper scissors (9)

These are – as their name suggests – only used for paper, in order to keep the blades sharp.

Tracing wheel (10)

This is used to trace a line from one piece of paper or pattern on to another directly underneath it.

Pattern master (11)

This is used to create lines and curves and to check angles.

Aluminium metre ruler (not shown)

This is essential for drawing and connecting longer, straight lines.

Silhouettes

First impressions of an outfit are created by its silhouette – the overall shape created by a garment. This is before qualities conveyed by the detail, fabric or texture of the garment can even be acknowledged, so the shape and form that a garment takes is a fundamental consideration in the design and construction processes.

The importance of silhouette

Silhouette is fundamental to the preliminary stages of the design process in order to determine which parts of the body will be emphasised and why. Once these decisions are made, it is up to the pattern cutter and designer to start contemplating how the design can be physically constructed and, if necessary, supported and structured using underpinnings and foundations. Many materials and techniques can be used to shape a silhouette (see chapter seven: Support and structure). For example, using shoulder pads to widen the shoulder can create an illusion of a small waist and narrow hips.

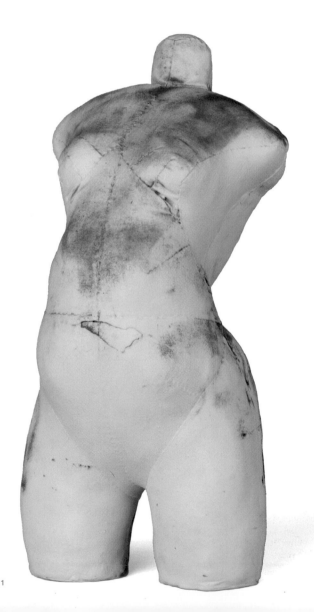

Proportions and bodylines

Proportion refers to the comparative relations and dimensions of the various parts of a whole outfit. A combination of garments can look messy or can work in harmony. For example, the ways in which a jacket, a skirt and a pair of boots relate to one another will add to the sense of proportion and balance conveyed by the outfit as a whole.

Proportions can be changed fairly easily using various construction methods. For example, moving a hemline, waistline, pocket, seam or dart position can dramatically alter the balance of width and length on an individual body shape. Choice of fabric texture and colour can also add to the overall effect conveyed by the cut and shape of a garment.

1   Sculptured ceramic mannequin by Helen Manley.

2   The changing shape and proportions of fashion in the Western world over the course of history.

2

1800

1830

1895

1900

1911

1912

1920

New Look, 1947

The change of silhouette over time

Throughout history fashion has always reflected the wealth of the nation and status of individuals. See pages 138–139 for a more detailed look at the history of supported and structured garments.

Pattern cutting tools and equipment > Silhouettes > Sizing and grading

Sizing and grading

Designs for a garment can be cut and made to fit an individual customer or they can be graded and altered to fit wearers of differing sizes. Either way, a full and detailed knowledge of sizing and grading is essential for any designer hoping to create a beautifully fitting garment. Being able to translate body proportions to paper and back to a three-dimensional garment takes much practice and careful attention to detail is fundamental.

1

Sizing

1   A flexible tape measure is essential for the sizing and grading process.

2   Technical drawing of a graded pattern piece.

Womenswear sizing is based on measurements of height, bust, waist and hips. In the UK, sizing starts at size 6 and goes up to size 22 (the best-selling sizes are 12, 14 and 16). European sizes start at size 34 (which is equivalent to size 6) and go up to size 52. American equivalents range from a size 2 to 18. However, as the fashion industry becomes increasingly sophisticated and complex, it is becoming much easier to find other size ranges to accompany these, such as Petite, Tall or Half-Size.

Menswear sizing is universally made up of a chest measurement for a jacket, and a waist and inside leg measurement for trousers. Shirt sizes are given by the neck measurement.

In childrenswear the principal variable is usually height so sizing is governed mainly by age.

Measurements for each size can be taken from charts in pattern cutting books but, where possible, it is always best to take real measurements from live models.

Grading

Grading is the process of scaling a pattern to a different size by incrementing important points of the pattern according to a set of given measurements, such as the British Standard sizing chart. Grading is a very specialised area in pattern cutting that not many professionals master. The secret is to know where the pattern needs changing to fit the decrease and increase in body size. Such increments can vary from 3 to 5cm (1.5–2in), depending on the garment range.

Many manufacturers use the British Standard sizing chart, which was first established in the 1950s and has changed over the years to accommodate changes in lifestyle. The United States has its own sizing chart and many other nations have worked out standard sizing for their own needs. Factors such as culture and diet have great influence on a country's average body shape. For example, northern European body shapes are generally tall and large whereas the average body shape in the Far East is shorter in height and slimmer in stature. For these reasons, a design house must always carefully consider the market it wants to sell to.

When grading a pattern, make sure that all corresponding seams, notches and punch marks match before starting the grading process. Grading can be done by hand with a metric grader's set square, pattern master or an L-square ruler, as well as by computer using a specific program, such as Lectra or Asys.

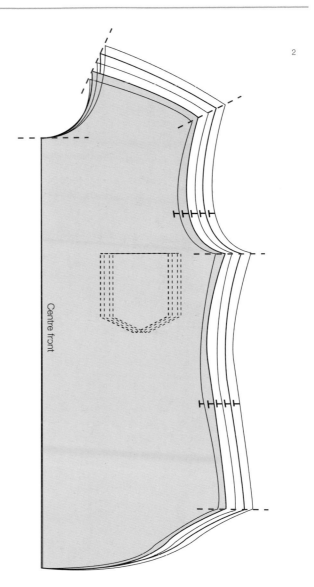

2

Centre front

Taking measurements

Neck girth (1)
This is the measurement around
the base of the neckline.

Shoulder length (2)
This is measured from the neckline
to end of shoulder bone.

Top bust girth (3)
This is measured around the body,
under the arm but above the bust
in a horizontal line.

Bust girth (4)
This is measured around the fullest
point of the bust in a horizontal line.

Under bust girth (5)
This is measured around the rib cage
under the bust in a horizontal line.

Waist girth (6)
This is the measurement around
the narrowest part of the waist
(natural waistline) in a horizontal line.

High hip girth (7)
This is measured around the
abdomen about 8–10cm below
the waistline in a horizontal line.

Hip girth (8)
This is the measurement around
the fullest part of the hip in a
horizontal line.

Arm length (9)
This is measured from shoulder
point, past the elbow, down to
the wrist with the arm slightly bent.

Front length (10)
This is measured from the
shoulder/neckline cross point,
past the nipple and down to the
natural waistline.

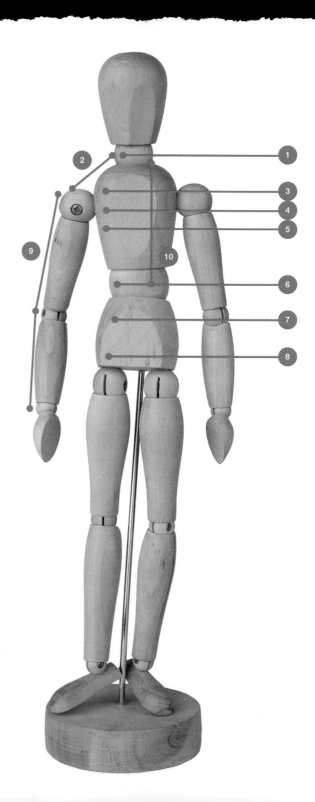

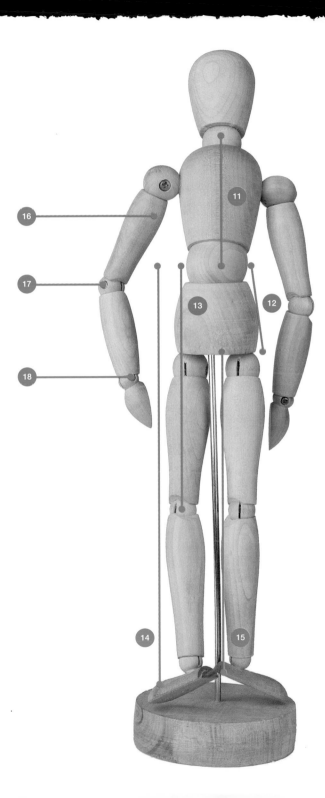

Back length (11)
This is measured from the nape
of the neck to the natural waistline.

Waist to hip (12)
This is the distance between the
natural waistline and the fullest point
of the hipline.

Waist to knee (13)
This is the distance between the
natural waistline and the knee.

Outside leg (14)
This is the distance from the natural
waistline to the floor or outside ankle.

Inside leg (15)
This is the distance from the inside
crotch to the floor or inside ankle.

Bicep (16)
This is the measurement around the
top of the arm.

Elbow (17)
This is measured around the width
of the elbow.

Wrist girth (18)
This is measured around the width
of the wrist.

When taking measurements,
make sure that the tape is
neither too loose nor too tight
around the body.

There are many more
measurements that can be
taken. If you are constructing
a shirt with a tight fitted
sleeve, for example, the
measurements of the bicep
(16), elbow (17) and wrist (18)
also need to be taken into
consideration. This is to avoid
the fit being too tight or too
loose on the arms.

Silhouettes > **Sizing and grading** > Blocks and patterns

Blocks and patterns

Blocks and patterns enable the designer to render something flat (paper or fabric) into something three-dimensional. They are laid on to fabric, cut out and assembled together using seams. In order to create well-made garments, it is essential that the designer fully understands the techniques used in order to make pattern cutting as straightforward and accurate as possible.

The block

A block (also known as a sloper) is a two-dimensional template for a basic garment form (for example, a bodice shape or fitted skirt) that can be modified into a more elaborate design. Blocks are constructed using measurements taken from a size chart or a live model, and do not show any style lines or seam allowance.

Blocks must, however, include basic amounts of allowance for ease and comfort; for instance, a tight-fitting bodice block would not have as much allowance added into the construction as a block for an outerwear garment might. A fitted bodice block would also have darts added into the draft to shape the garment to the waist and bust, whereas a block for a loose-fitting overcoat would not need these.

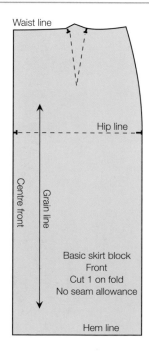

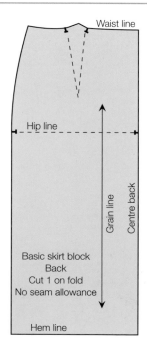

The pattern

A pattern is developed from a design sketch using a block. The designer or pattern cutter will add to the block by introducing style lines, drapes, pleats, pockets and other adjustments to create an original pattern.

The final pattern features a series of different shaped pieces of paper that are traced on to fabric and then cut out, before being seamed together to create a three-dimensional garment. Each pattern piece contains 'notches' or points that correspond to a point on the adjoining pattern piece, enabling whoever is making the garment to join the seams together accurately. The pieces need to fit together precisely, otherwise the garment will not look right when sewn together and it will not fit well on the body.

When the block modification is finished, seam allowance is added to the pattern. To perfect a pattern, a toile (a garment made out of a cheap fabric such as calico) is made and fitted on to a live fitting model. Adjustments can be made on the toile before being transferred to the pattern. This stage is examined in more detail on page 58.

1   A sample skirt block.

2   The translation to pattern.

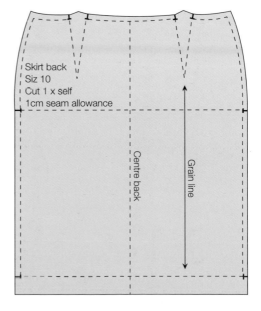

Skirt waistband
Size 10
Cut 1 x self + blk fuse
1cm seam allowance

Fold line

Grain line

Centre front   Side seam   Centre back

Skirt front
Size 10
Cut 1 x self
1cm seam allowance

Centre front

Grain line

Skirt back
Siz 10
Cut 1 x self
1cm seam allowance

Centre back

Grain line

2

Samples
A sample is the first version of a garment made in real fabric. It is this garment that goes on the catwalk or into a press/showroom. Samples are produced for womenswear in sizes 8–10 to fit the models. Once the sale book is closed, the samples are stored in the company's archive. Some samples of past collections are taken out by designers for photo shoots, events such as premieres and for reference or possible inspiration for future collections.

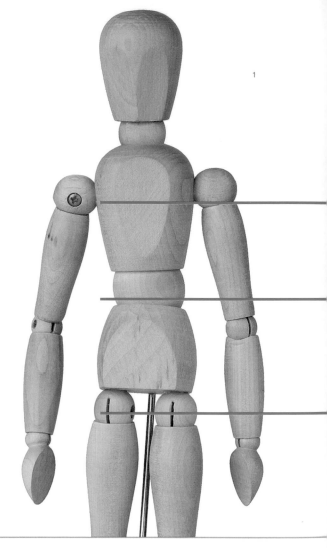

1

How the measurements relate to the block

Whether taking individual measurements or using a size chart, the main measurements (bust girth, waist girth, waist-to-hip length and hip girth) will give a good indication of the body shape the design is intended to fit.

Secondary measurements may also be taken from an individual or from a size chart. This may be the length of skirt, for example, when drafting a skirt block.

Darts can be used to control excess fabric and to create shape on a garment when stitched together. Curves are added to create shape depending on the nature and purpose of the block.

1   The block and its corresponding measurements.

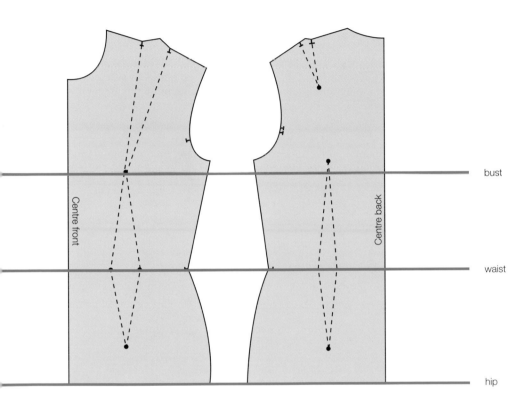

Centre front

Centre back

bust

waist

hip

How to start a set of blocks

A set of blocks can be cut for one individual in order to create bespoke/couture garments. Design houses will often create their own set of blocks to complement their special ethos and design philosophy. When starting a set of blocks, it may help to ask the following questions:

Who is my target group: women, children or men?

What will be the smallest and the largest size in my size chart?

What is my sample size?

What is my collection range: lingerie, tailoring, streetwear?

The answers to these questions will make it much easier to cut the right blocks from which to create original patterns for each collection.

> *'I use the same approach to clothes as I did when I designed buildings. It is basic geometry: you take a flat form and revolve it in space.'*
>
> Gianfranco Ferre

1   Meadham & Kirchhoff
A/W07.
Catwalking.com.

Like all craft skills, pattern cutting can at first seem difficult and intimidating. But with a basic understanding of the rules to be followed (and broken!) the aspiring designer will soon learn interesting, challenging and creative approaches to pattern cutting. To draw the right style line in the correct position on a garment takes experience and practice. Designers who have been cutting patterns for twenty years can still learn something new – the process of learning never stops. This makes creative pattern cutting a fascinating process.

In this chapter we introduce the meaning of a drafted block and how to turn it into a pattern from a design drawing. We take a look at dart manipulation as well as pocket, collar and sleeve construction. You will be introduced to cutting techniques and bias-cut garments. You will also learn about the fitting process: how to fit the toile and alter the pattern accordingly. Finally we take a look at the different ways of laying and cutting patterns from fabric.

How to read a design drawing

1/2 Photograph and illustration of design by Karin Gardkvist.

3 A basic bodice block.

This is the point at which pattern cutting becomes much more creative and exciting. Once the design has been completed, the process of breathing life into a flat design drawing in order to achieve an actual garment can begin. To be able to achieve a beautiful garment shape takes time and experience. Remember nothing ever happens without practising your skills – don't be disheartened if it doesn't work first time round. All outstanding fashion designers and creative pattern cutters have worked for years to perfect their skills.

1

2

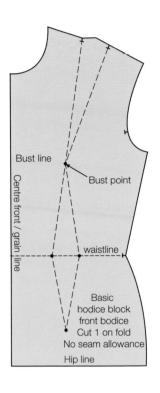

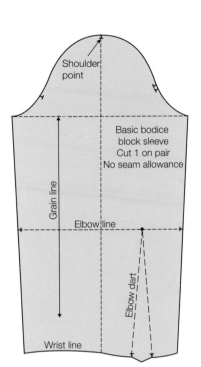

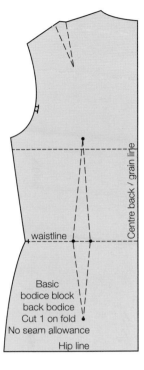

Bust line

Bust point

Centre front / grain line

waistline

Basic
bodice block
front bodice
Cut 1 on fold
No seam allowance

Hip line

Shoulder point

Basic bodice
block sleeve
Cut 1 on pair
No seam allowance

Grain line

Elbow line

Elbow dart

Wrist line

waistline

Centre back / grain line

Basic
bodice block
back bodice
Cut 1 on fold
No seam allowance

Hip line

3

Translating drawing to block

The translation of a design drawing to pattern requires an eye trained for proportions. Most design drawings are sketched on a figure with distorted proportions. The legs and neck are too long and the figure too slender. These sketches are often inspiring and wonderful to look at but unfortunately give a false image of the human body and it is a key task of the pattern cutter to address this.

How to mark the block

It is essential when cutting a block or a pattern that the correct information is supplied. A bodice block, for example, has to show the horizontal lines of the bust-, waist- and hiplines. Parts of the block such as the waist and bust points should be notched or punch marked (holes and notches indicate where the separate pieces of fabric will be attached to one another) and the grain line must be indicated. This will clearly show the position in which the pattern should be placed on the fabric. Additional information must be written clearly in the centre of the block, including whether it is a front or back piece, a tight- or loose-fitted bodice block and the sample size, preferably with the measurements and any allowances to be made when constructing the block.

Once the pattern has been constructed the seam allowance can be added. Seam allowance can vary in size from a narrow 0.5cm for a neckline (to avoid having to clip or trim the seam) to 2.5cm in the centre back of trousers (to be able to let some out if the waist gets too tight). Seams that are to be joined together should always be the same width. Mark the width of the seam allowance on the block.

Usually, the block ends up being divided into further pattern pieces. At this point, therefore, the information should be reconsidered accordingly, except the grain line and front or back information, which are always transferred to the new pieces.

How to read a design drawing > Dart manipulation

Marking symbols on a pattern

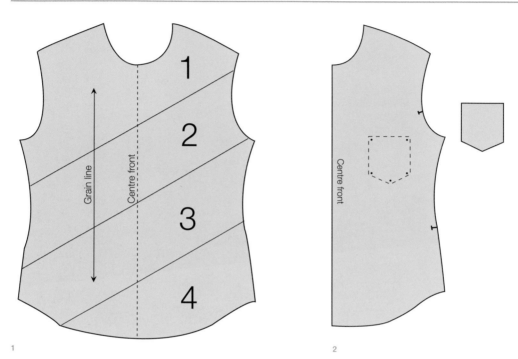

1

2

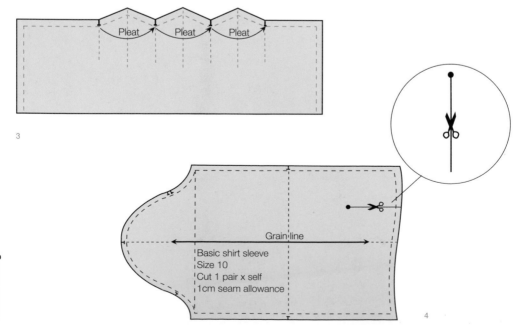

3

Basic shirt sleeve
Size 10
Cut 1 pair x self
1cm seam allowance

Grain line

4

5

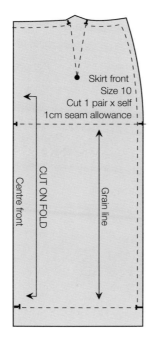
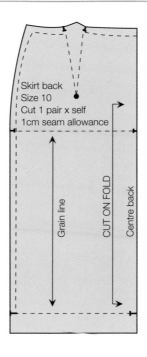

Skirt front
Size 10
Cut 1 pair x self
1cm seam allowance

Centre front
CUT ON FOLD
Grain line

Skirt back
Size 10
Cut 1 pair x self
1cm seam allowance

Grain line
CUT ON FOLD
Centre back

1   Number sections before cutting a pattern apart to avoid confusion.

2   Position marks, such as for pockets, are hole punched into the pattern.

3   Marking the direction of pleating helps to avoid confusion.

4   Cutting lines are best marked with the symbol of a pair of scissors.

5   If the piece is to be cut on the fabric fold (so it does not have a seam), indicate this with the message 'cut on fold'.

6   Cut 1 x self (or cut 1 x) = cut the one piece only
Cut 1 pair x self (or cut 2 x) = cut two pieces
C.F. = centre front
C.B. = centre back.

6

Skirt waistband
Size 10
Cut 1 x self + blk fuse
1cm seam allowance

Centre front
Grain line
Side seam
Fold line
Centre back

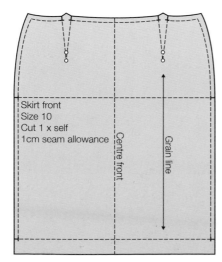
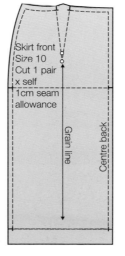

Skirt front
Size 10
Cut 1 x self
1cm seam allowance

Centre front
Grain line

Skirt front
Size 10
Cut 1 pair
x self
1cm seam
allowance

Grain line
Centre back

How to read a design drawing > Dart manipulation

Dart manipulation

1   An asymmetrical design with intersecting darts.

2   Gianni Versace, A/W07. Catwalking.com.

Darts control excess fabric to create shape on a garment. They can be stitched together end to end or to a zero point also known as the pivotal point (such as the bust point). Dart manipulation is the most creative and flexible part of pattern cutting. The possibilities are endless and the designer's imagination is the only limitation. Darts can be turned into pleats, gathers or style lines. Their positioning on the body is very important; not only do these techniques create fit, shape and volume, they also change the style and design of the garment.

Example of dart manipulation on a bodice block

Design analysis: asymmetrical design with intersecting darts coming from the waist and ending at the bust point.

1. Trace bodice block on fold. When copying the left side of the front block, transfer the complete waist and bust dart into the armhole. Then copy the right side of the front block on to the left front block (centre front attached to centre front) and transfer the complete waist and bust dart into the armhole.

2. Draw in the slashing lines according to your design.

3. Cut along the slash lines, up to the bust point (pivotal point), Close up the darts and tape them down.

4. Add seam allowances and mark the dart ends with a hole punch as well as notching the position of the left dart, centre front and seam allowances. Mark the gain line (in this case the centre front) and add information such as 'front, right-side-up, cut 1 x'.

5. If required, the armholes and neckline can be altered for more comfort. A back pattern can be cut to fit the front design.

6. The pattern is now ready to be cut out of calico and made into a toile for a fitting.

1

Slash and spread

1 Skirt constructed by slash and spread method to gain flare.

2/3 Asymmetric skirt that has been opened up on one side only.

This method is used to add extra volume and flare. The technique involves creating slash lines that reach from one end of the pattern to the other, sometimes ending on a pivotal point like a dart ending. These slash lines will then be opened up for added volume and flare.

Using slash and spread techniques

Slash and spread techniques can be used to convert a straight skirt pattern into a skirt with flare. The most basic way of doing this is to divide the pattern up into equal pieces from hem to waist and open them up by equal amounts all the way round. Redraw the hemline in a smooth curve.

To create asymmetric flare, as shown in 2 and 3, the pattern is divided into two and slash lines are marked on to one of these halves. These are cut along from hem to waist and opened up (spread) with equal amounts added into each 'slash'. This creates flare on one side of the skirt. Pleats have also been added to the waistline. Drawing in an angular hemline creates the asymmetric point.

Tip
When using the slash and spread method remember that the position you slash in is the exact position the fabric will flare out. So when slashing into one side only, the flare will not spread across but only appear on one side.

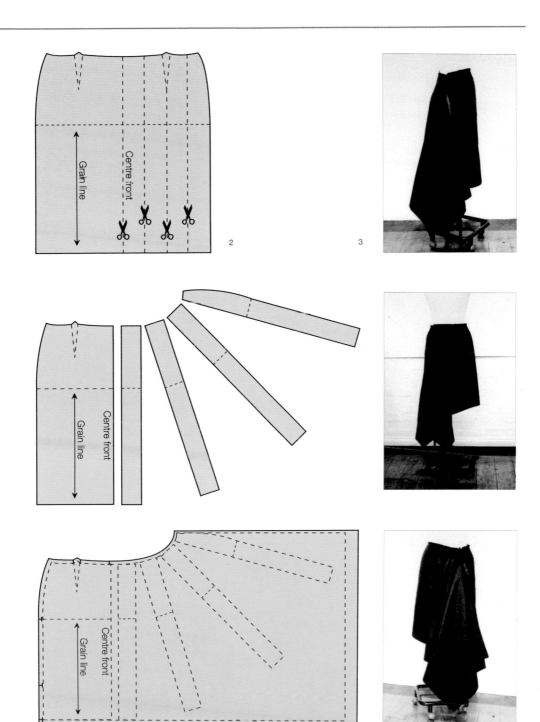

Grain line

Centre front

2

3

Grain line

Centre front

Grain line

Centre front

Sleeves

1   Christian Dior, haute couture, S/S07. Catwalking.com.

2   A sleeve block for a set-in sleeve, showing the part where the sleeve can be eased into the armhole.

3   Variations on the one-piece set-in sleeve:

a   Peak sleeve.

b   Cap sleeve.

c   Leg o' mutton sleeve.

d   Juliet sleeve.

e   Trumpet sleeve.

f   Bishop sleeve.

Sleeve construction is a very special part of pattern cutting. Sleeves can be part of the bodice (laid-on sleeve) or set into an armhole (set-in sleeve). Without any other design features added, a garment can look outstanding by simply creating an interesting sleeve design. The most basic sleeve block is the one-piece (set-in) sleeve, which can be varied as shown in 3a–f (facing page). Different sleeve blocks can be developed from the one-piece block, such as the two-piece sleeve and laid-on sleeves, including raglan, kimono/batwing and dolman designs.

2 Ease

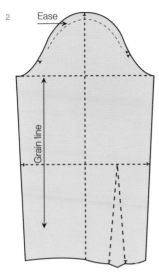

Grain line

3a

3b

3c

3d

3e

3f

Constructing sleeves

When constructing a set-in sleeve, the measurement of the armhole is essential. Therefore, the bodice front and back are constructed first and once the measurement of the armhole is established, ease is added according to the type of block (jacket block, fitted bodice block and so on). Ease is added to a pattern to allow for extra comfort or movement. As well as allowing the sleeve to sit comfortably in the armhole, ease will also affect the fit and silhouette of a garment. Ease is distributed between the front notch and the double back notch of the sleeve (see technical drawing above). In some set-in sleeve designs, the ease is taken across the shoulder to achieve a round appearance over the shoulder point. A sleeve is sitting comfortably in the armhole when it aligns exactly with, or is set slightly in front of, the side seam of the bodice.

One-piece and two-piece sleeves

There are differences between one-piece and two-piece sleeves, the major one being the amount of seams that are used. A one-piece sleeve has only one seam placed under the arm at the side seam position. Therefore, the seam cannot be seen when the arm is relaxed. The two-piece sleeve has two seams; one is placed at the back, running from the position of the back double notch down to the wrist, past the elbow. The second seam is moved a little to the front, from under the arm side seam position (still not visible from the front). The look of a two-piece sleeve is more shapely and it has a slight bend to the front. As such, it is possible to get a closer fit with a two-piece sleeve because of its extra seam. One-piece sleeves are used for a more casual look, whereas two-piece sleeves are mostly seen on garments such as tailored jackets or coats.

Laid-on sleeve

The laid-on sleeve is part of the bodice. Once constructed, either a part of the armhole remains or there is no armhole at all.

A laid-on sleeve is most commonly constructed by separating the one-piece sleeve through the shoulder notch straight down to the wristline to gain a front piece and a back piece (see technical drawing below). The next step is to align the front piece of the sleeve with the bodice's front shoulder and the back sleeve with the bodice's back shoulder. From this point onwards several styles can be developed, such as batwing or kimono, raglan, gusset and dolman sleeves. The sleeve can be laid on at variant angles – the greater the angle, the more excess fabric and therefore a greater range of arm movement.

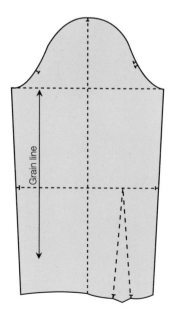

1

Grain line

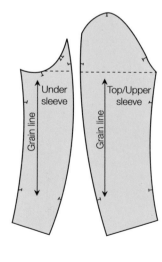

2

Under sleeve

Grain line

Top/Upper sleeve

Grain line

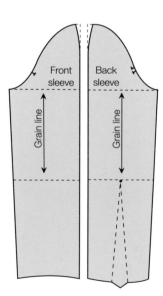

3

Front sleeve

Back sleeve

Grain line

Grain line

Gusset sleeves

To extend the lift (a technical term for moveability of the arm) in a sleeve a gusset can be added. A gusset is traditionally a diamond-shaped piece, which is inserted into a slit in the underarm section of the sleeve.

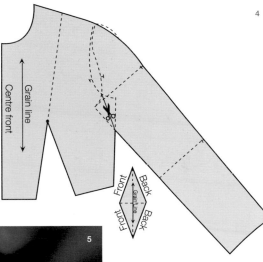

4

5

1   Basic one-piece sleeve.

2   Basic two-piece sleeve.

3   Basic split sleeve.

4   Gusset sleeve construction.

5   Christian Lacroix, A/W07.
    Catwalking.com.

Slash and spread > **Sleeves** > Collars

Kimono sleeves

Like a Japanese sleeve, the kimono
sleeve is cut in one with the bodice.
The seams can run from the outer-
or underarm.

1   Alexander McQueen, S/S08.
      Catwalking.com.

2/3/4 Preparation for a kimono
      sleeve construction.

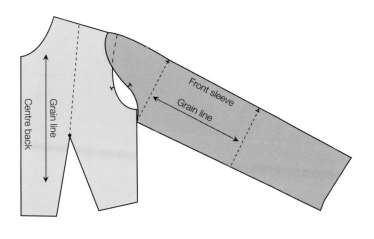

Back sleeve
Grain line

Grain line

Centre back

2

Grain line

Centre back

Front sleeve
Grain line

3

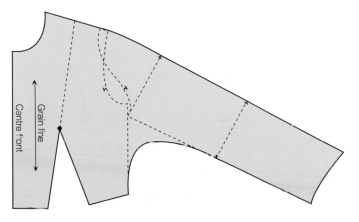

Grain line

Centre front

4

Raglan sleeves

The raglan sleeve has a dropped shoulder design. It is constructed to have a seam running from the neckline on a slant into the underarm on front and back.

Lord Raglan
Lord Raglan was a commander of the British troops during the Crimean War. His right arm was injured at the Battle of Waterloo and had to be amputated. As a result he got himself a coat designed with a special sleeve – the raglan sleeve.

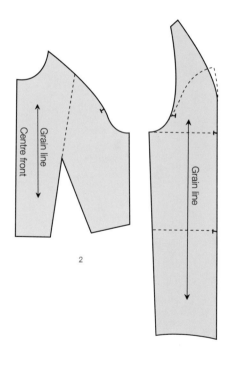

1   Trench coat with raglan sleeve.

2   Raglan sleeve construction.

3   Example of a dolman sleeve.

4/5/6 Dolman sleeve construction.

Dolman sleeves

Originally named after the 1870s
coat/wrap that looks like a cape from
the back with lowered armholes and
set-in sleeves in the front. The dolman
sleeve today has lots of fabric under
the arms and can be fitted to the
wrist, still looking like a cape from
the back. The sleeve construction
is illustrated in 4–6. The original back
bodice construction (4) shows the
laid-on sleeve. The final pattern
pieces show the front bodice that
has been extended underarm (5)
and the back bodice with the
laid-on sleeve (6).

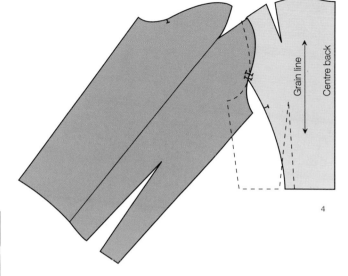

Grain line

Centre back

4

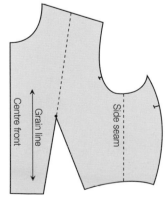

3

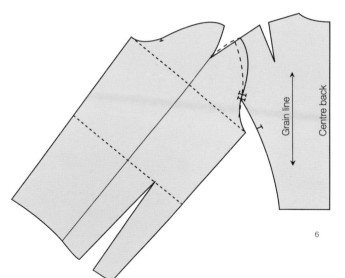

Grain line

Centre back

6

Centre front

Grain line

Side seam

5

Pleated, darted and gathered sleeves

The one-piece sleeve block can be adapted in countless ways. These patterns illustrate how the sleeve block can be altered to create puffed, pleated and darted sleeves.

1

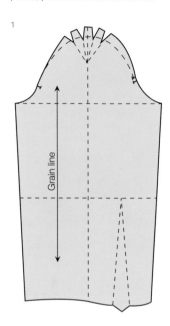

Grain line

2

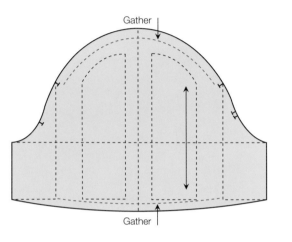

Gather

Gather

Cuff

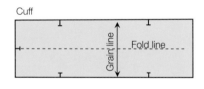

Grain line   Fold line

3

4

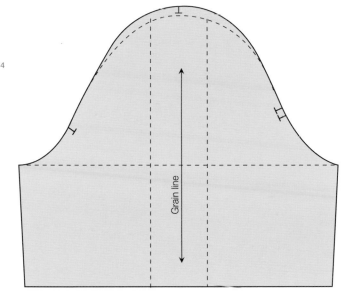

Grain line

1   Pattern construction of
    a darted sleeve head.

2   Pattern for a puff sleeve
    construction with gathers
    on the sleeve head and
    small cuff.

3   Jacket with a darted
    set-in sleeve by Hugo Boss,
    S/S 08.

4   Preparations for a pleated
    sleeve head construction.

5   Pattern construction of
    a pleated sleeve head.

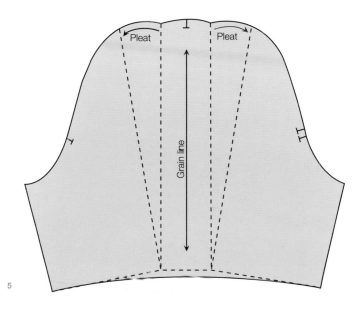

Pleat   Pleat

Grain line

5

Collars

The collar is a versatile design feature that will enhance the style of a garment. It is attached to the neckline of the garment and allows the size and shape of the neckline to vary. Collars come in all shapes and sizes and the most common are the stand-up/mandarin, shirt, flat, sailor and lapel collar constructions.

1

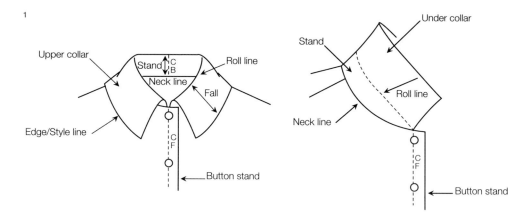

Drafting variations

1   Technical drawing showing the key elements of a basic collar construction.

2   A right-angle collar.

3   Flat collar on a pea coat.

Collars can be constructed in three basic ways. The first method is a right-angle construction, used for stand-up collars, shirt collars and small flat collars such as Peter Pan and Eton collars.

Secondly by joining the shoulders of the front and back bodice together to construct the collar directly on top of the bodice block. This technique is used to construct sailor collars and bigger versions of flat collars. The advantage of using this method is that the correct outer length of the collar construction results automatically, however large the collar or neckline extension is.

Finally, the lapel construction, which is extended from the centre front, from the breaking point toward the shoulder. By extending the break/roll line a collar construction can be added. A version of this is the shawl collar, where the collar extends from the fabric of the garment on to the lapel without being sewn on.

Basic collar measurements

The measurement of the neckline on
the pattern has to be taken in order
to construct a collar. Therefore, if the
neckline is to be changed according
to the design, do this before cutting
the collar pattern.

2

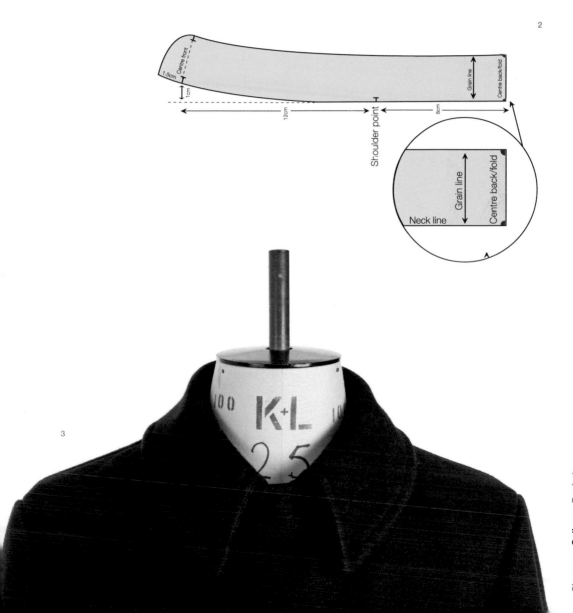

3

Right-angle construction collars

Right-angle collars are constructed
by drawing the centre back line and
the neckline at a right-angle to each
other and adding all measurements.
Variations of this basic construction
include mandarin or stand-up collars
and shirt collars, which can have
either integrated or separate stands.

Example: ½ neck size = 20cm (Back neck length = 8cm/Front neck length = 12cm) Button stand allowance 1.5cm

Basic stand-up collar   1

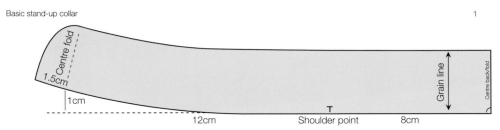

Tighter fitting stand-up collar

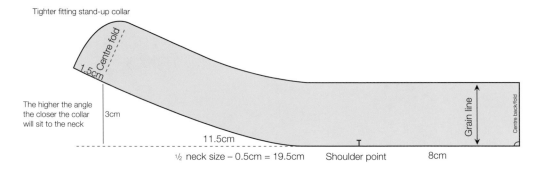

Stand-up/mandarin collars

If the centre front of the collar is
constructed higher than the neckline
and the centre back point, the collar
will sit close to the neck. If the centre
back of the collar is constructed
higher than the neckline and the
centre front point, the collar will sit
away from the neck.

Flat collars

A flat collar, with or without a stand construction included, traditionally meets in the centre front without an over- and under-wrap (the over- and under-wrap is an extension from the centre front to create space for the button and buttonhole). The collar has a small stand height (generally between 0.5 and 1.5 cm) and lies comfortably along the shoulder.

1   Stand-up collar. The shorter the top edge of the collar, the closer the fit.

2   Menswear jacket with a stand-up collar by Courtney McWilliams.

3   Peter Pan collar pattern.

4   Eton collar pattern.

3   Example: ½ neck size = 20cm (Back neck length = 8cm/Front neck length = 12cm)

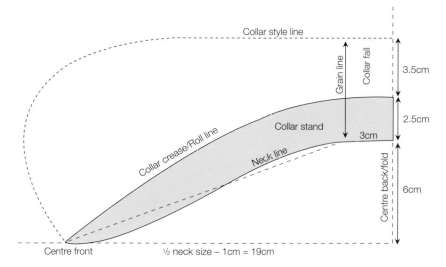

Example: ½ neck size = 20cm (back neck length = 8cm/front neck length = 12cm)

The collar fall should never be more than double stand width.

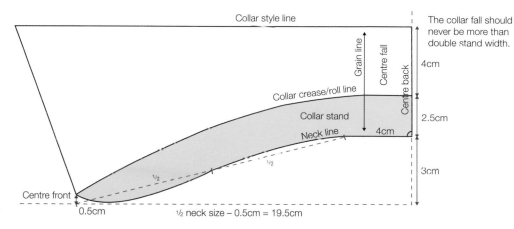

4

Shirt collar

A shirt collar stand can either be separate or integrated into the collar construction. Integrated stands are used for smaller shirt collars.

1

Example: ½ neck size = 20cm (Back neck length = 8cm/Front neck length = 12cm) Button stand allowance 1.5cm

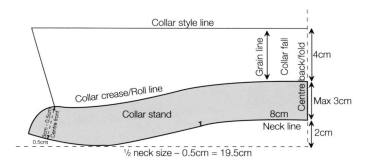

Shirt collar with separate stand

A shirt collar with a separate stand is closer to the neck than a collar with an integrated stand. A separate stand allows the designer to build more height into the construction, creating a more severe and military looking collar.

2

Example: ½ neck size = 20cm (back neck length = 8cm/ front neck length = 12cm). Button stand allowance 1.5cm

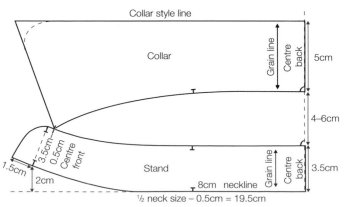

A collar drafted with a separate stand sits closer to the neck than a collar drafted with an attached stand. The stand width can be any size on a separate collar! A basic stand width is 2.5.

1   Shirt collar construction.

2   Shirt collar with separate stand construction.

3   A shirt collar with separate stand.

4   Shirt with shirt collar by Peter Jensen, S/S08. Catwalking.com.

Button-down collar
The button-down collar is a variation of the shirt collar. Its design was inspired in England at a polo match where the players had their collars attached to keep them from flapping in the wind. The 'button-down' can be worn informally with the collar open as well as dressed up with a tie or bow-tie.

3

4

Collars joined at the shoulder

This shape of collar was originally copied from the naval uniform. The look is traditionally a V-shaped neckline in the front and a long square panel that lies flat down the back. The sailor collar construction is used not only to cut the sailor style but also for other big collar shapes.

1/2/3/4   Sailor collar construction.

5   Donna Karan, SS/08. Catwalking.com.

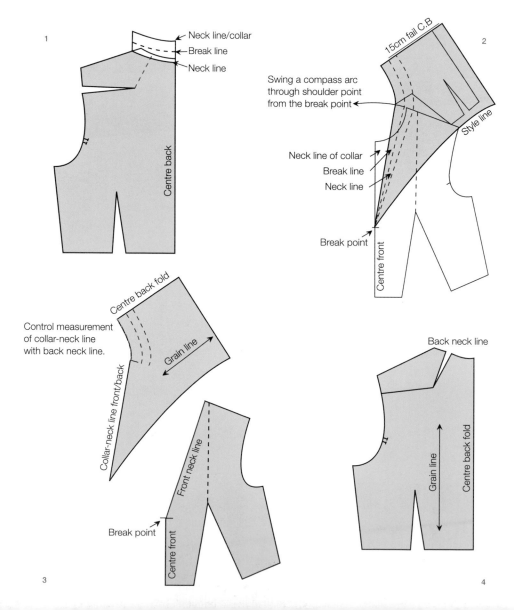

1

Neck line/collar
Break line
Neck line

Centre back

2

15cm fall C.B

Swing a compass arc through shoulder point from the break point

Style line

Neck line of collar
Break line
Neck line

Break point

Centre front

3

Control measurement of collar-neck line with back neck line.

Centre back fold

Collar-neck line front/back

Grain line

Break point

Centre front

Front neck line

4

Back neck line

Grain line

Centre back fold

Tailored collar

A lapel collar is a V-shape neckline
with the lapel grown on. The
extension (the lapel) is folded back
and reveals the facing. It is the front
section of a jacket, coat, blouse or
shirt. The lapel is usually joined to a
collar and both can be cut in various
shapes. A variation of a lapel is a
shawl collar, a construction whereby
the lapel and collar are joined
together.

Before a lapel can be constructed,
the designer must establish the
position of the breaking point and
also whether the garment is to have
a single- or double-breasted style.

1/2   Double-breasted lapel collar
construction.

3/4   Single-breasted lapel collar
construction.

5   Top- and under-collar
construction.

1   2

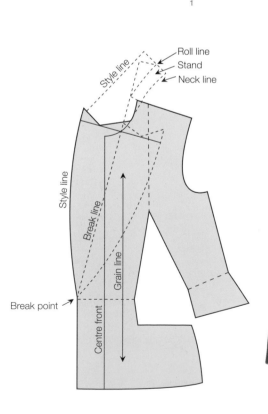

Roll line
Stand
Neck line

Style line

Style line

Break line

Grain line

Break point

Centre front

3

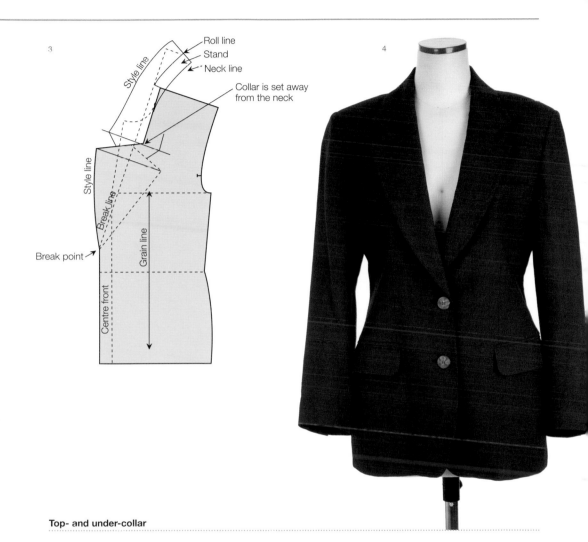

Roll line
Stand
Neck line

Collar is set away from the neck

Style line

Style line

Break line

Break point

Centre front

Grain line

4

Top- and under-collar

A tailored collar can be constructed in two parts: the lapel and collar. The collar has a top layer (the top-collar) and an underside layer (the under-collar). The top-collar should be bigger in size with added millimetres around the edges of the under-collar (2–3mm on a fine to middleweight fabric and 4–5mm on a thicker fabric). The top-collar is made bigger to prevent the under-collar from showing beyond the stitching line.

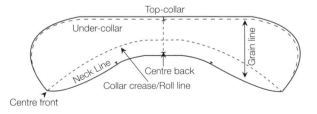

Top-collar

Under-collar

Neck Line

Centre back

Collar crease/Roll line

Grain line

Centre front

5

Pockets

1   A variety of pocket styles used on casual wear.

2   Womenswear jacket with box pleat pockets and flaps.

3   Levi's jeans with trademark pocket.

4   Hugo Boss jacket with pleated patch pockets.

5   Menswear jacket with jetted pockets and large pocket flaps.

6   Womenswear jacket with jetted pockets.

Before the fifteenth century, pockets were simply pouches worn attached to a belt. It was not until the mid-eighteenth century that dressmakers started to introduce small pockets into the waistline seams of dresses. These days pockets are not only traditional and functional, they can also be used to define the style of a garment. Pockets fall into two basic categories: patch pockets, where the pocket bag sits on the outside of the garment; and set-in pockets, where the pocket bag is set inside the garment. The set-in pocket opening may be hidden or made into a design feature.

Designing pockets

Pockets should be functional, so try to create pockets that are large enough to put a hand in. Remember that men's hands are larger than women's.

Some tailors add a pleat in the centre of the inside pocket bag to allow for shaped objects, such as keys, to go inside the pocket bag without pulling and showing a stretch mark on the jacket outside.

The position of the pocket on the garment is very important. Not only is it a focus point, it also needs to be easily accessed. The best way to find the pocket position is to fit the garment on a life model and ask him or her to point out a comfortable position for the pocket mouth.

When grading a garment with pockets, make sure to grade the pocket within natural proportions.

3

2

4

BUNKA

BUNKA

5

6

When using slant, continental or side seam pockets in trousers, make sure to continue the pocket bag into the centre front zip fly. This method will keep the pocket bags in place and create a nice finish in the inside of the garment.

When constructing welt or jetted pockets in the back of trousers or skirts, sew the pocket bag into the waistband for stability.

The pocket mouth (this is the part where the pocket is worked in) should always be secured through an interlining.

Inside pockets sometimes have buttons to enable the pocket bag to be closed. Cover the button up with a triangular piece of lining, to avoid the button leaving marks on garments worn under the jacket. It also prevents the button from being caught in the garment underneath.

Go around twice when you stitch up the pocket bag and use a small stitch (2–2.5mm) for extra strength.

Bias cut

1   Jean Paul Gaultier
     haute couture, S/S07.
     Catwalking.com.

2   Construction of a cowl
     collar.

3   Menswear shirt with
     cowl collar.

Madeleine Vionnet was the first designer to introduce bias-cut garments successfully. Women exchanged their girdles for bias-cut dresses that draped across their bodies and showed off their natural shape. Bias-cut garments are cut at 45 degrees to the straight grain of the fabric. For more information on fabric grain, see pages 64–65.

How to create bias-cut garments

• Choose the right fabric for the garment: crepe, crepe de chine, satin crepe, georgette, silk and chiffon are all perfect for the job.

• Bias-cut garments should be cut on a true bias, 45 degrees from the straight grain of the fabric.

• For the fabric to hang properly the true bias must run through the centre of the panel (centre front and centre back).

• Some bias cuts depend on the fabric hanging longer on one side; cross grain is not twisted as tight as straight grain and therefore falls more easily on the bias.

• Fabric on the bias moves easily. To control the fabric, use a layer of tissue paper underneath and pin together. Trace the pattern pieces on to a sheet of paper the same size as the fabric and pin all layers together. Use sharp scissors to cut out the pieces.

1

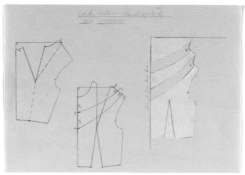

2

3

- Always do some test stitching to find the right machine and stitching type. An overlocking seam works well as it will allow the seam to stretch.

- All garments cut on the bias create fitting problems, therefore it is important to have fittings in order to reduce excess fabric created by the stretch of the bias. A combination of drafting and draping is essential when working on the bias.

- The best way to fasten a bias-cut garment is with a zip. Use a tape and hand tack the zip first before using the sewing machine.

- It is often best to cut the facings for bias-cut garments on the straight grain and to tape necklines, armhole and shoulders.

- A pin hem is a nice hem finish. However, if you would prefer a rougher look use a raw edge.

The cowl collar

Cowls are drapes that fall in soft folds off the shoulder point and drape along the front neckline or back. The folds are created using a true bias cut and the pattern can be constructed on the flat or by draping on a mannequin. Some cowls are designed with pleats or gathers with varying numbers of folds. Cowls can either be cut in one piece with the garment or as a separate piece.

Fitting the toile

1   Vivienne Westwood menswear jacket at development stage and the final outcome presented at the fashion show.

All garments should be properly fitted before going into production and a number of methods can be employed to do this. When creating bespoke garments, the toile will be fitted on the customer in person. However, designs that are created for a design house or high street store will most likely be fitted on a house model or a mannequin stand.

Carrying out a fitting

A designer will produce a 'toile' for the first fitting. This is a garment made out of a cheaper fabric close in weight and behaviour to the final fabric, such as calico. Calico is a cheap cotton fabric and comes in different weights: lightweight for blouses and shirts; medium for jackets and trousers and heavy for coats or sculptured pieces. A toile has no finished seams, no fastenings, nor any lining or facings.

At the first fitting the designer looks at the proportions and fit of the garment. Only once the overall shape has been established does the attention turn to the details. Such details might include the position of pockets, belt loops, collar size and other detailing. These will usually be marked with a tape, marker pen or pinned-on fabric pieces.

A well-fitted garment should complement the design and the body shape. As such, it is best to fit on a live model so that it is possible to see the movement of the garment. The most difficult areas of the body to fit are the armhole and sleeve, the trouser crotch and around the bust area. Before starting with the pattern construction make sure that you use a well-fitting block to avoid unnecessary fitting problems and always construct your pattern on the large side. It is easier to fit a toile by adjusting the shape to the body than it is to start opening up seams and patching in sample fabric to make it bigger.

The choice of fabric is important as it needs to reflect the quality of the final fabric used. If working on a woven style, use a calico in the right weight. Again, for jersey/knitwear garments, use a jersey of the right weight. When cutting out the toile make sure to cut in the right grain line; if the garment is meant to be cut on the bias then the toile needs to be cut on the bias too. The different grain lines make the garment drape differently on the body. The toile should always be made out of an unpatterned, light-coloured fabric as this shows off the seams and details of the garment in the best possible way.

Tips for the first fitting

When preparing for a toile fitting some parts of the garment can be hand sewn, for example, the sleeve into the armhole. The rest of the toile should be sewn together with a bigger machine stitch (3–4mm), as it is easier to unpick the toile after the fitting if necessary.

Mark all the lines necessary for a fitting, for example centre front and back, waist and hip line, elbow line. These lines can be marked with a pen or thread.

If using shoulder pads, use the same pair as for the final garment. The same applies to any underpinnings such as underskirts and corsetry.

The collar can be fitted without an under-collar attached in the first fitting, as it makes it easier to fit for a better shape.

Pocket positions can be drawn on in the fitting. It is easier to find the right position with the live model as they can attempt to put his or her hands into the pocket. If pocket flaps or patch pockets are used, cut out shapes of the sample fabric ready to be pinned on in the fitting.

If the final fabric has a pattern, draft parts of it onto the toile to show off detailing.

All seams or darts on the toile need to be pressed out really well and in the same order as on the final garment.

Bias cut > **Fitting the toile** > Laying a pattern on to fabric

Further fittings

Any alterations that have been made since the first fitting will be revisited in the second fitting. The detailing will be looked at and discussed. Decisions about finishes such as binding or top-stitching are finalised. Once everyone is happy with the fit, the garment can be cut out in the final fabric and a shell fitting can take place.

The shell fitting enables the designer to see how the final fabric behaves on the body. As such, the garment is only very basically constructed. The seams are not cleaned up and facings and lining are not yet attached. If necessary, small alterations can still take place at this stage.

Sometimes more than one or two toile fittings take place, especially on new shape developments. Fittings are time-consuming and cost money but they are necessary for a well-proportioned and well-fitting garment.

Altering the pattern

Alterations are tricky and cannot be ignored, as a badly fitted garment will not sell. Whether we are tall, short, small or big the high street is offering a more diverse collection to choose from and customers will not accept a badly fitting outfit.

1   Christian Dior fitting a house model.

Fitting example of a set-in one-piece sleeve

2   **The look:** the sleeve shows horizontal lines that pull across the sleeve head, which look like a pleat.

3   **The correction:** the head of the sleeve (also called the scye) is too long. Pin across the sleeve head where the pleat is showing or pin away the extra fabric on the top of the sleeve head/scye. Then correct on the pattern by folding away the paper in the same way that the fabric sleeve was pinned. Re-cut the sleeve and fit it again on a model.

2

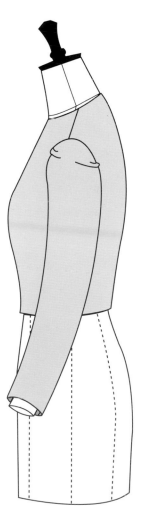

3

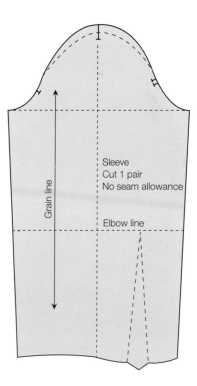

Grain line

Sleeve
Cut 1 pair
No seam allowance

Elbow line

Fitting example of a set-in
one-piece sleeve

4   **The look:** the sleeve shows
     a diagonal pulling from the
     back to front on the sleeve
     head area.

5   **The correction:** the shoulder
     notch is not in the right
     position. The sleeve needs
     to be turned in by a certain
     amount, between 0.5 and
     2cm, depending on how
     much the sleeve is pulling.
     Change the position of the
     shoulder notch and try the
     same sleeve in the armhole
     using the new shoulder
     notch as a guide.

4

5

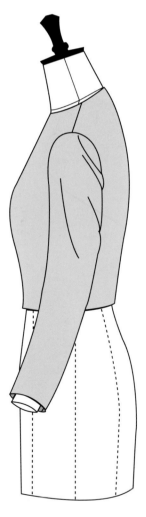

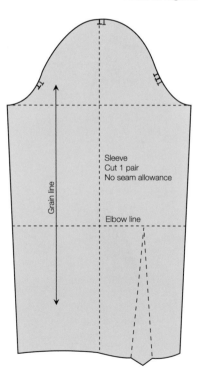

Grain line

Sleeve
Cut 1 pair
No seam allowance

Elbow line

Fitting example of a set-in
one-piece sleeve

6   **The look:** the sleeve shows
     diagonal pulling from bottom
     to top at the front and back
     of the sleeve.

7   **The correction:** the scye of
     the sleeve is too short. By
     taking fabric from the sleeve
     head, the sleeve should fit in
     the armhole. Pin along the
     scye seam until the sleeve
     falls straight down from the
     armhole. Take the amount
     pinned off the sleeve from
     the underarm position of
     the sleeve pattern.

6

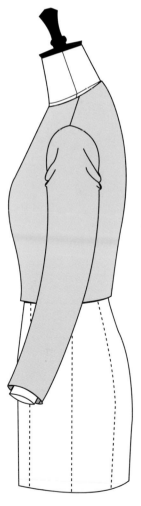

7

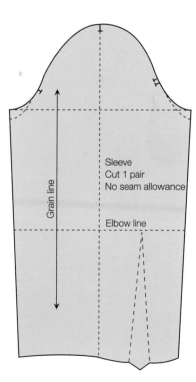

Sleeve
Cut 1 pair
No seam allowance

Grain line

Elbow line

Laying a pattern on to fabric

1   The cut of a garment in
relation to the direction of
the grain line can strongly
affect how the fabric hangs
on the body.

It takes time and patience to cut out a pattern in fabric. Taking time
to prepare for cutting and marking the fabric pieces guarantees a
better result when putting the garment together. It is also helpful to
have a firm understanding of fabrics and weaving techniques. For
more information on the specific qualities of various fabrics see
Basics Fashion Design: Textiles and Fashion.

What is a grain line?

A material is woven using a yarn
going lengthways (the warp) and
crossways (the weft). The lengthways
edge of the fabric is called the
selvedge. The cut of a garment in
relation to the direction of the grain
line will strongly affect how the fabric
hangs on the body. There are three
ways of cutting the grain:

Straight grain – this is the most
common method, whereby the
grain line of the pattern pieces is
parallel to the selvedge. The yarn
used lengthways (warp) is a
stronger yarn than the one
used crossways (weft).

Cross grain – this method uses
pattern pieces that are cut at a
90-degree angle to the selvedge.
Pieces that are cut crossways are
most likely to be decorative, for
example cuffs, yokes, collars
and complex shapes, such as
a whole circle skirt.

Bias – for a true bias cut, pattern
pieces are cut at 45-degree angle
to the selvedge and cross grain.
Garments cut on the bias are lively
and drape beautifully around the
body but will take up a lot more
fabric.

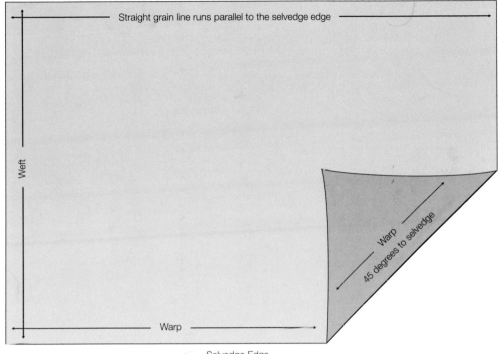

Selvedge Edge

Straight grain line runs parallel to the selvedge edge

Weft

Warp

Warp
45 degrees to selvedge

Selvedge Edge

1

Preparing the fabric

Examine the fabric carefully before cutting out the pattern pieces. There are some elements to watch out for:

Does the fabric need pressing before cutting?
Wool: pure wool (or fabric that contains wool fibres) shrinks and therefore needs to be steamed with an iron before it is cut out.

Cotton/linen: fabric from cotton or linen fibre that has not been treated needs to be pressed with steam to shrink it and to press all the creases out before cutting.

Silk: silk does not shrink but still benefits from a good press to get rid of the creases. This makes it easier to cut the pattern out. Use a dry iron on silks (without steam).

Synthetics: synthetics do not crease much and do not shrink. Press slightly without steam.

Does the fabric have a direction?
Nap: a nap can be on one or both sides of the fabric. The fibre ends stick out on the surface of the fabric, making it soft to the touch. These fabrics, such as velvet, corduroy, fur, brushed cotton, should be cut in one direction only.

Shine/colour: some fabrics have a shine or change colour when they are looked at from different angles.

Which are the good and the wrong sides of the fabric?
When buying a fabric from the roll, the good side is usually facing the inside of the roll. If buying a piece of

fabric with no clear indication, go with whichever side is preferable or by looking at the selvedge. Any needle holes in the selvedge or marks where the holes have been punched through indicate the wrong side of the fabric.

Does the fabric have straight edges and does it need straightening out?
Look at the fabric on the table. Some fabrics need to be pulled by hand in both directions to be straightened out. To get a straight crossways line, pull one of the weft threads by hand as a guiding line and cut along the pulled thread.

Layout of the pattern – cutting plans

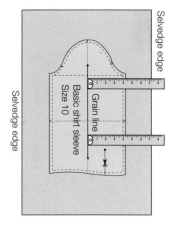

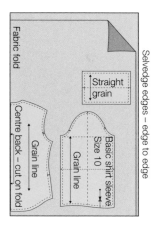

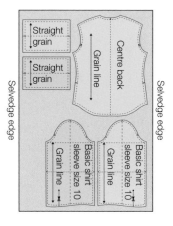

Laying the pattern pieces on the correct grain line

To place the pattern pieces correctly on to the fabric, use the grain line information on your pattern (the long arrow through the pattern). Once you have decided which direction to place the pattern, make sure that the grain line is parallel to the selvedge on the fabric. To ensure that the pattern piece is laid correctly, measure from both ends of the arrow/grain line out to the selvedge.

Double layout

This is the easiest cutting plan of all. The pattern is constructed one side only (one front piece, one sleeve, one back piece, etc) and indicated with the message 'cut 2 x' or 'cut a pair'. Some pattern pieces are half of a pattern with a folding line and the cutting instruction 'cut on fold' (half of collar, half of yoke). The fabric is folded exactly in half by placing one side of the selvedge on to the other side throughout its length. The pattern is then laid on to the fabric as economically as possible. The pieces can be laid in any direction if the fabric has no shine or nap.

Single layout

For this layout the pattern has to be copied open (the whole of the front or back) and indicated with the cutting instruction 'cut 1 x or cut 1 self'. This cutting plan is used when the pattern pieces are asymmetric or the fabric has a pattern design. The fabric is placed openly with the selvedge to the right and the left running down lengthways. The pattern pieces should be laid in one direction if there is a one-way design on the fabric.

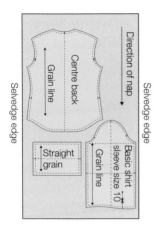

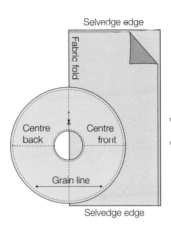

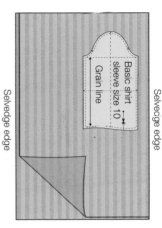

Layout for fabric with a nap or one-way design

This can be cut out as a single or double layout. Decide on the direction of the nap or design of the fabric and mark the top of the fabric. Then place all the pattern pieces in one direction, running from the top downwards along the selvedge.

Crossway layout

This method is used when the pattern pieces are complex shapes and do not fit any other way, for example a whole circle skirt. Instead of folding the fabric along the long side, the fabric is folded crossways with the selvedge on each side touching. A fabric with nap needs to be cut along its folding line into two pieces. Turn one layer around – wrong side facing wrong side of the fabric – so that the nap runs in the same direction.

Cutting out checks and stripes

Before cutting the fabric ascertain whether or not the check or stripe pattern is symmetrical. You can use the double layout or the single layout when the pattern is symmetrical. When using the double layout make sure you match up by pinning the checks or stripes together every 10cm. This will avoid mismatch of the check or stripe pattern on symmetric pieces such as sleeves and front pieces. It is important that the adjoining pattern pieces match up with the pattern on the fabric. Therefore mark the dominating bars/stripes on to the pattern and then match up on to the adjoining pattern piece. The parts to watch out for are the side seams, centre front and back, armhole and sleeve, pockets, facings, cuffs, yoke and collar.

Marking the pattern on to the fabric

The pattern can be marked on to the fabric once you have decided which cutting plan to use. First the pattern pieces are weighed down and/or pinned on to the fabric and aligned with the grain line. It is best practice to mark around the paper pattern before lifting it off. This helps to avoid cutting into the paper pattern when cutting the fabric. However, it is essential to transfer all information necessary for constructing the garment on to the fabric pieces. There are different ways to do this:

Chalk marks
Using a tailor's chalk to mark certain positions such as dart endings and pocket position is easy and not very time consuming, but be careful that the chalk mark cannot be seen on the good side of the fabric.

1   Chalk marks.

2   Transferring the pattern to fabric.

3   Thread marks.

1

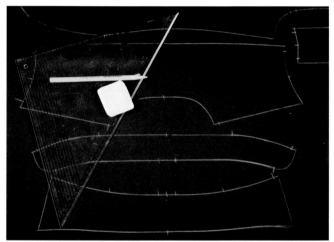

2

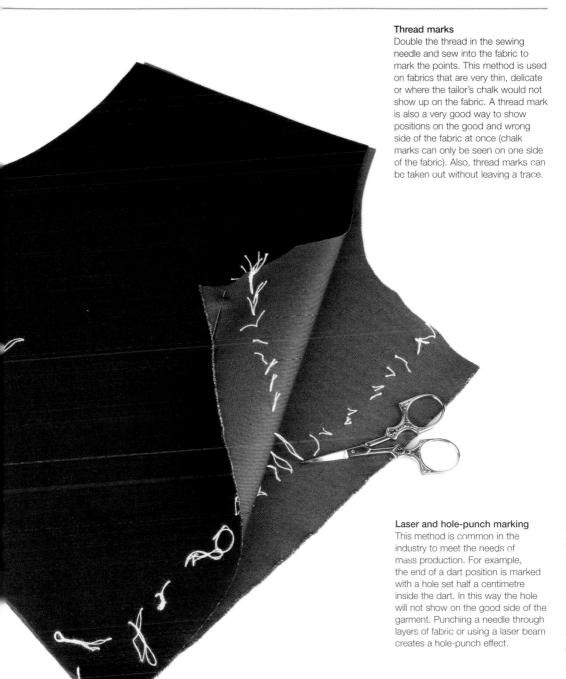

Thread marks

Double the thread in the sewing needle and sew into the fabric to mark the points. This method is used on fabrics that are very thin, delicate or where the tailor's chalk would not show up on the fabric. A thread mark is also a very good way to show positions on the good and wrong side of the fabric at once (chalk marks can only be seen on one side of the fabric). Also, thread marks can be taken out without leaving a trace.

Laser and hole-punch marking

This method is common in the industry to meet the needs of mass production. For example, the end of a dart position is marked with a hole set half a centimetre inside the dart. In this way the hole will not show on the good side of the garment. Punching a needle through layers of fabric or using a laser beam creates a hole-punch effect.

Fitting the toile > Laying a pattern on to fabric

'What I do is restricted by the cloth and the human body.
My job is to make that cloth give expression to the body.'

Vivienne Westwood

**This chapter introduces the different tools and machinery used
to construct a garment. It will look at the numerous techniques
available to hand sew or machine stitch a range of fabrics, and
will take a closer look at the history of haute couture and the
tailoring crafts.**

**Garment construction can be divided into different specialised
areas. At the top of the manufacturing chain are haute couture
and the tailoring crafts, which involve working with individual
customers. At the lower end of the manufacturing chain are
industrially produced garments. In contrast to tailoring and
haute couture, garments produced in this way are much
quicker to manufacture. A lot of the work is mass produced
by machinery and time-efficient construction methods.**

**This chapter looks at the various tools and materials used
to construct garments and provides an introduction to
hand sewing and machine sewing techniques.**

Tools for the technique

The following equipment is used in the construction of garments. You will find the necessary items for hand and machine sewing in most haberdashery shops. If you are looking to invest in industrial machinery then talk to a tradesman first (for further information see the list of contacts on page 188).

Fabric scissors/shears (1)
Depending on the weight and thickness of the fabric, different kinds of shears can be used. Look for a medium-size pair of scissors for normal use and another larger pair for heavier fabric. It is important that the scissors/shears lie comfortably in your hand, so try them out before buying them. You should always go for the best quality you can afford when buying a cutting tool. To prolong their life, fabric scissors should only be used on fabrics.

Hand-sewing needles (2)
There is a big variety of sizes, shapes and points to choose from. For most purposes use a medium length (37mm), thin sewing needle with a round eye.

Tape measure (3)
You should have one hanging around your neck at all times when sewing together a garment, in order to take control measurements throughout the process.

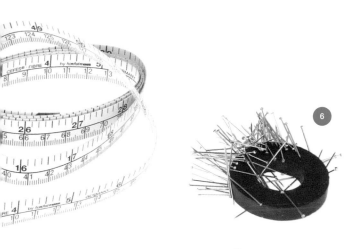

Embroidery scissors (4)

These scissors are small and sharp with pointed blades. They are good to use for small detail cutting or to snip threads.

Tailor's chalk (5)

This chalk comes in several colours and can be brushed off after application. There are also wax/synthetic chalks available in white and black. These come off when pressed over by a hot iron.

Pins (6)

Pins come in different sizes and materials. Stainless steel, 35mm dressmaking pins are pleasant to handle. When working with knitwear, use safety pins – normal pins will disappear into the garment.

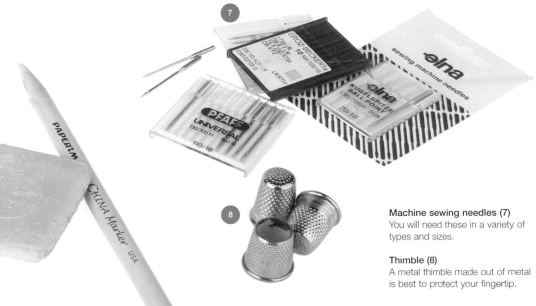

Machine sewing needles (7)

You will need these in a variety of types and sizes.

Thimble (8)

A metal thimble made out of metal is best to protect your fingertip.

Tools for the technique > Seams

Pressing equipment

Point pressing block (1)

Good to use on small, sharply angled areas such as cuffs and collars.

Needle board (2)

The board has fine needles very close together and is used to press fabrics such as velvet, corduroy and brushed fabrics while protecting the nap or pile.

Tailor's ham (3)

A firmly stuffed cushion that will help to press round shaped parts or seams on a garment (for example around the bust area).

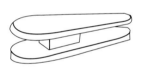

Sleeve board (4)

A narrow, padded board for long, straight seams. Perfect to use on a sleeve once the seams are closed down.

Bobbin and bobbin case for industrial sewing machines.

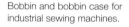

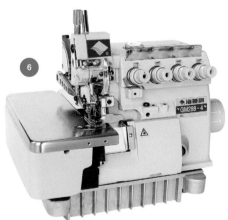

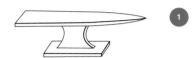

Machinery

Industrial flat bed machine (5)
This machine can sew any type of fabric using a basic straight stitch.

Overlocker (6)
Overlocking stitches are used to protect the edges of a fabric. They can be made up of three, four or five threads and the type of fabric dictates which to use. An overlocking stitch is a series of threads that combine to lock the fabric along its edge. A blade runs along the edge of the fabric chopping off excess material and threads.

Coverstitch (not shown)
A coverstitch machine is used in the construction and finishing of jersey fabrics and for lingerie. Twin needles create two rows of stitching on the right side of the fabric and an overlocking stitch on the wrong side. A variation of this stitch creates an overlocking stitch on both sides of the fabric. Unlike an overlocking

machine, this machine does not cut off excess fabric.

Buttonhole machine (not shown)
This machine creates two kinds of buttonhole: a 'keyhole' and a 'shirt' buttonhole. Shirt buttonholes are the most common type. Keyhole buttonholes are mainly used on tailored garments, such as coats and suit jackets.

Industrial iron and vacuum table (7)
An industrial iron is heavier and more durable than a domestic iron and the steam has a higher pressure. It can be used with a vacuum table, which is shaped like an ironing board and often has a smaller board for ironing sleeves. A pedal underneath the machine allows the user to create a vacuum while ironing; the air and steam are sucked through the fabric into the bed of the machine. This reduces the steam in the atmosphere

and also holds the fabric to the ironing board, allowing for easier pressing.

Pressing is essential to a garment; fabric will crease and rumple as it is handled and manipulated under a machine. Unpressed seams do not lie flat and the garment will look unfinished if it is not ironed.

Fusing press (8)
A fusing press is the industrial machine used to attach (melt) iron-on interfacing to fabric. It is more efficient and durable than an industrial iron.

Zip foot for concealed and one/both-sided zips.

Teflon foot and universal sewing machine foot.

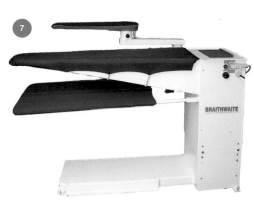

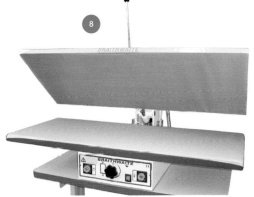

The right thread for the job

These days there are threads in all sorts of colours and thicknesses, for all kind of jobs. The material to spin a thread can be natural (cotton or silk) or synthetic, such as polyester. Cotton thread is used primarily for cotton, linen or wool fabric, whilst silk thread is used for silk or woollen fabrics. This is also a beautiful thread for most kinds of hand sewing, as it glides through any type of fabric. The polyester thread can be used for both natural and synthetic fabrics.

1

2

3

4

5

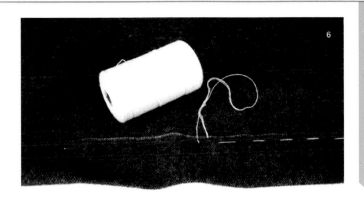

6

Tacking thread is a loosely twisted cotton thread that breaks easily. It is used for basting stitch, a temporary stitch that can be removed when it is no longer needed.

7

9

8

10

1 A selection of threads.

2 Thread on cones.

3 Silk thread on spools.

4 Cotton thread.

5 Wool and linen yarn on card.

6 Tacking thread and basting stitch.

7 Metallic thread.

8 Decorative yarn in bundles.

9 Top-stitching yarn.

10 Nylon thread.

Seams

Seams are the most basic way of joining two or more pieces of material together in garment construction. Seam allowance is added; this usually faces the inside of a garment but varies according to the type of seam used. Seams are also used to create shape and have an impact on the design of the garment. Some seams are used to strengthen parts of a garment (in corsetry, for example) while others are there simply for design purposes. There are some points to consider when choosing the right seam for constructing a garment. Different fabrics and styles require different seams. You will find various styles of seam to choose from and it is always possible, of course, to create your own.

Getting started

The seams introduced here are made using a sewing machine. There are two ways of preparing a seam. One is to place the pieces of material together, using pins to hold them in place. The other (safer) way is to place the material together and hold in place with a hand basting stitch running along the stitching line (see page 85).

Once the material is ready to be taken under the machine, start the stitching process by taking a couple of stitches forward and then secure the stitching by going back in the same line and forward again. When coming to the end of the seam, repeat by going back a couple of stitches and then forward again. This will secure the sewing line. Also make sure that any hanging threads are neatly cut off before moving on to the next stage.

1

Running/plain seam

This kind of seam is the most basic and common version, with seam allowances ranging 0.5–2.5cm.

- Place two pieces of material together with the right sides facing and use a basting stitch to hold the seam allowance together.

- Use a flatbed sewing machine to sew the seam, creating a straight line of stitches.

- The length of the stitch can be changed on the sewing machine from 1mm to 5mm (basic stitch length is 2.5–3mm).

- The seam allowance can be overlocked or bound to stop the edge from fraying.

- This seam can be pressed open or to one side.

1   Machine-stitched tunnel on the bottom of a jacket.

2   Running seam used to attach two pieces of fabric.

3   Running seam pressed open with an iron.

4   Overlocked seam allowance pressed open.

5   Overlocked seam allowance pressed to one side.

2
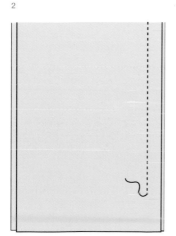

3
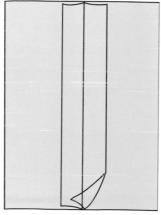

4

5
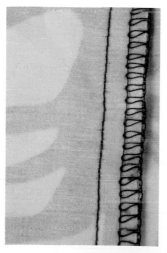

French seam

1   Technical drawing of a French seam.

2   Wrong side of the fabric showing a French seam finish.

3   Good side of the fabric showing a French seam finish.

4   Technical drawing of a flat fell seam.

5   Good side of a flat fell seam on a jeans trouser.

6   Technical drawing of a welt seam.

The French seam creates a neat finish and is primarily used for transparent and fine fabrics. It is the favourite of the couture atelier (from where it originated). The seam allowances are cut 1.2cm in total.

• To start, place the wrong sides together. Take a 0.5cm seam allowance and stitch a seam on the right side of the fabric.

• Then turn the seam inside out, placing the right sides of the fabric together. Stitch the seam, taking 0.7cm seam allowance and encasing the previously stitched seam.

• Press the seam to one side.

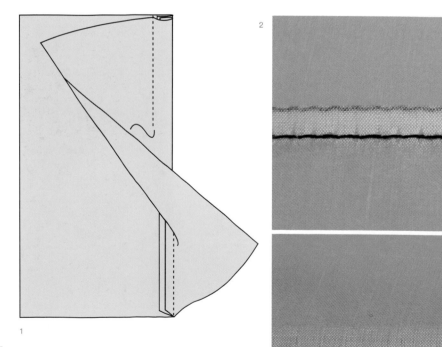

1

2

3

Flat fell seam

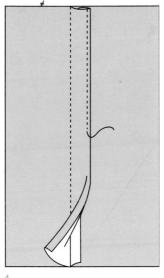

4

The flat fell seam is popular on denim garments, men's shirts and work wear. It is a hardwearing, strong self-enclosed seam. It shows two rows of stitching on the right side and one row of stitching on the wrong side of the garment. The seam allowance is 0.7cm on one side and 1.7cm on the other.

• Place the wrong sides of the fabric together. Move the piece with the 0.7cm seam allowance 1cm further in from the other piece.

• Sew a seam taking the 1.7cm seam allowance from the outer edge.

• Then fold over the 1cm extra allowance to cover the 0.7cm allowance and press flat.

• To finish off, top-stitch 1–2mm from the folded edge (edge stitch).

5

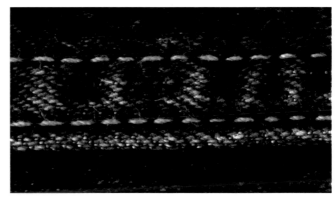

6

Welt seam

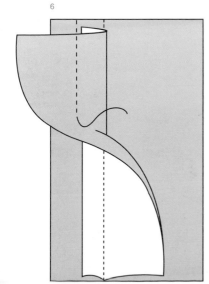

A welt seam can be confused with a top-stitched seam, but when looking closer, the seam shows a distinct ridge on one side. The welt seam is one of the strongest seams and is used in garments such as designer tailored wear or denim wear. Depending on the preferred width of the welt cut, the seam allowance is 1.5cm for a finished welt width of just under a centimetre.

• Put the right sides together and sew a straight line, taking a 1.5cm allowance.

• Press the seam to one side.

• Trim off a couple of millimetres from the enclosed seam allowance.

• With right side up, top-stitch to enclose the trimmed edge.

Seam finishes

1   Overlocked seam.

2   French seam.

3   Centre back seam with a bound seam finish.

4   Prada dress with bound edges on collar, front and sleeve, S/S08. Catwalking.com.

5   Technical drawing of an open pressed seam allowance with bound edges.

The raw edge of a seam allowance usually needs treating to stop the fabric from fraying. The technique used to finish a seam allowance depends on the style of garment and the budget. Here are some options to choose from:

The easiest and cheapest way to clean up an edge is to overlock the edges using a three or four-thread coverstitch machine.

French seams are a seam and seam finish in one. They are more time consuming and therefore more expensive, but provide a clean way to finish off fine and transparent fabrics.

Bound seam allowances are popular on half-lined jackets or jackets without a lining and on trouser seams.

1

2
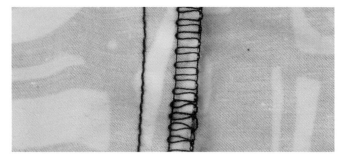

3
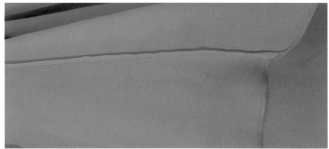

Edge and seam finish with a binding

Any raw edge such as a hem, neckline or seam allowance can be finished with a binding. Bindings are strips of fabric that can be cut to any width. When using a woven fabric as a binding, cut the fabric on the true bias grain line. Bindings are visible on both sides of the garment.

- Prepare the edge by cutting off the allowance (except if you are binding seam allowances).

- Cut a strip off the chosen fabric four times the width of the finished binding.

- Press the binding strip lengthways in half, with the wrong sides together.

- Open the strip up and fold both long sides in to meet the pressed centre line and press again.

- Now take the raw seam edge and wrap the binding strip around it and pin in place. The centre pressing line of the binding is now aligned with the raw edge of the garment.

- Put under the sewing machine and top-stitch the binding down at the right side of the garment, through all layers with an edge stitch, catching both binding edges at the same time.

4

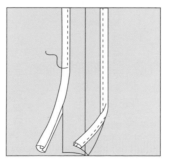

5

Hand sewing techniques

1 Technical drawing showing how to secure the thread at the beginning and end of hand stitching.

2 Lace fabric and organza sewn together with a basting stitch.

3 Technical drawing of a blind hemstitch.

4 Blind hemstitching on a hemline of a dress.

5 Technical drawing of a cross-stitch.

Sewing machines are now highly sophisticated and can handle a whole range of very specific sewing tasks. However, there are skill areas in garment construction which, either by choice or simply because there is no other way, are better addressed with hand sewing. Hand sewing can be relaxing and often helps to create a special bond between you and the garment. It is important to use the right needle and thread and also to use a thimble to protect your finger. Sit on a good chair with a foot rest so you don't have to bend over your work and do not arch your back too much. Make sure you work in good light. Always sew towards yourself and do not cut your thread too long, as it gets in knots. Furthermore, do not pull the thread too tight, as this will show on the outside of the garment.

Getting started

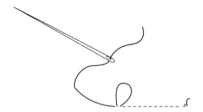

First make sure that the thread has a small knot on the end. Begin your hand sewing with a backstitch. Pick a tiny bit of fabric at the starting point. Pull the thread with the knot through the fabric and do another stitch at the same point to create a loop. Pass the thread back through the loop, to secure the knot and prevent it from slipping out.

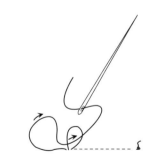

1

Basting stitch

Basting is used to temporarily join together parts of garments. The stitches are large, applied without tension and made using tacking thread in a contrasting colour. This process, also known as tacking stitch or running stitch, starts with a larger backstitch without a knot. It is not secured at the end, making the stitches easily removable. Basting is also used to join the edges of two identical pieces of fabric, such as organza and satin-duchess, so the fabrics can be used as one piece.

2

Hemming stitches

Hemming stitches can be used for any kind of hemming (joining two layers of fabric), for example on trouser, sleeve or skirt hems. The stitch is invisible from the outside of the garment and shows very little of the thread on the inside hem.

Woven fabrics

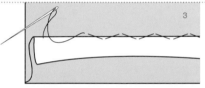

3

Blind hemstitching

*   Fold approximately 0.5cm of the hem edge back and use a blind hemstitch to sew from the inside of the garment.

*   Take a thread or two from the outer fabric (make sure that the thread cannot be seen on the outside of the garment) and make a tiny stitch from the hem.

*   Space the stitches about 1cm apart. The hemming edge can be overlocked for a flat finish.

*   The hem can be underpressed (underpressing is using the iron between the hemming and outer fabric). This means that the shiny line that can sometimes appear after pressing will not show through to the outside of the fabric.

4

Jersey fabric or knitwear

5

Jersey and knitwear fabrics have a natural stretch. If it is necessary to finish the hemming lines by hand make sure that the stitches are not restricting the stretch of the fabric. A cross-stitch hem, also known as a 'figure-eight' hem or 'catch-stitch' hem, has more stretch than a regular blind-stitched hem and is therefore perfect for use on jerseys and knitwear.

If necessary, the hemming edge can be overlocked before starting the hand stitches.

Cross-stitching

*   Turn the garment inside out and fold the hem allowance over by 0.5cm.

*   Work from left to right.

*   Secure the hem allowance, then catch one or two threads of the outer fabric.

*   Next take a tiny stitch in the hem and continue the process. Create a crossover with the stitches, leaving 0.7cm between each one.

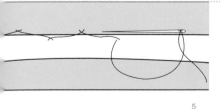

Seam finishes > Hand sewing techniques

Transparent fabrics and silks

1   Technical drawing of a
    slip-stitch.

2   Silk scarf with roll hem and
    slip-stitch finish.

3   Use a slip-stitch to attach a
    lining to a hem.

4   Lining attached to a hemline
    of a jacket.

5   Technical drawing of a
    prick-stitch.

6   A zip sewn into a dress
    using prick-stitching.

To achieve an invisible hem finish, use
a roll hem and slip-stitch technique.
This kind of hand stitch is common
on silk scarves and the cuff openings
on blouses made of delicate fabrics
but it can be used on anything that
requires a fine edge finish.

• Secure the thread with a knot
  and a backstitch at the
  starting point.

• Then turn the edge under by
  rolling the fabric inwards to
  the inside (wrong side) of the
  garment. You will create a tiny
  roll by doing so.

• Pick a thread from the outer
  fabric, making sure the thread
  is not seen on the outside of
  the garment.

• Then slip the needle directly
  above it into the turned/rolled
  edge and through the roll by
  a couple of millimetres.

• Come out of the roll and take
  another thread directly below
  from the outer fabric. Now
  repeat the process and make
  sure that no thread is visible
  from the outside or inside of
  the garment.

• When rolling the edge over,
  make sure not to take too
  much fabric in, as it is a
  refined finishing method.
  Using a thin needle and fine
  thread will make the job easier.

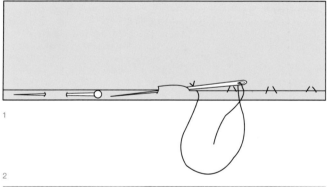

1

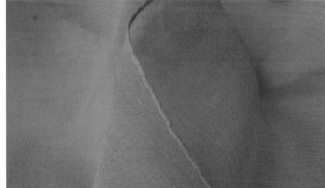

2

Linings

When working on a jacket, attach the hem of the jacket first with a blind hemstitch and then get the lining ready to be attached to the hem. The lining ends about 2cm above the jacket hem and is cut with extra length for a fold to provide lengthways ease (see 'Linings' on page 166).

Fold the lining 1cm over on the hem edge and pin to the jacket hem 1cm below its edge. You can use either slip-stitching or prick stitching to attach the lining.

Slip-stitching

- Secure your thread at the starting point and catch a small amount of fabric from the jacket hemming only.

- Avoid taking fabric from the outside of the jacket.

- Then immediately at the point of coming out of the fabric, slip into the lining for a couple of millimetres and come out with the needle to catch another small amount of the jacket hem. Continue from right side front to left side front and remember the jacket is inside out.

Prick-stitching

- The prick-stitch is similar to the slip-stitch but it is a stronger version of the two. The difference is that when applying the stitch into the jacket hem, the prick-stitch needs to go back on itself (backstitch) before slipping into the lining.

- This stitch can also be used for sewing in zips.

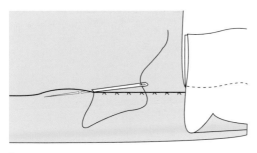

3

5

4

6

Other stitches

Other stitches can be used for decorative effects or to secure weak points on a garment.

1 Using a blanket stitch technique as a decorative edge finish on a wool fabric.

2 An overcast stitch.

3 Wool fabric with overcast stitch to prevent the raw edge from fraying.

4 An arrowhead tack.

5 A fagotting stitch.

6 A version of a hand-sewn fagotting stitch used as an edge finishing.

Blanket stitch

- Blanket stitch is a decorative stitch that can also be used to finish a raw edge.

- Choose the depth and length of your stitch and insert the needle vertically, keeping the same distance and depth throughout.

- Working from left to right, pass the needle through from back to front and bring the needle through the thread loop.

- Make sure that the knot lies on the top of the fabric edge.

1

2

Overcast stitch

- Overcast stitch is used to finish a raw edge.

- Work from right to left.

- Push the needle through the fabric edge from the back to the front, taking a 2–3mm stitch.

- Take the needle pointing left and create slanting stitches of the same distance and depth over the fabric edge.

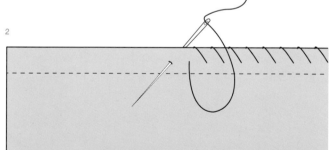

3

Arrowhead tack

Specific stitches are used to secure a weak point on a garment. Use an 'arrowhead' or 'cow's-foot tack' for example, to reinforce parts that may be under a lot of strain such as a split in a skirt, the ends of a pocket or the tops of pleats.

• Mark the position of the triangle with thread or chalk. Use a buttonhole thread and secure the thread with a knot.

• Starting on the lower left corner, push the needle through from the wrong side to the right side.

• Working on the right side of the fabric, tack the needle through the top point of the triangle, taking a tiny stitch.

• Then take the needle to the lower right corner and complete a stitch from the lower right corner to the lower left again.

• Continue this process from right to left, with stitches close together, until the triangle is complete.

4

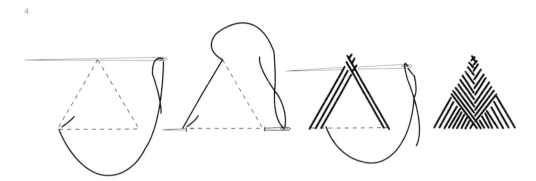

Fagotting stitches

Some decorative hand stitches can be used to join two fabric edges together, such as the 'fagotted seam'. This is an embroidery stitch that creates an open lacy effect.

• Start by drawing parallel lines on a piece of paper in the desired width of the fagotting.

• Turn both sides of the adjoining raw edge under. Tack these two edges on to the paper lines.

• Then start fagotting the two edges together by taking slanted stitches from one side to the other and pass the needle under each slanting thread to create a crossover.

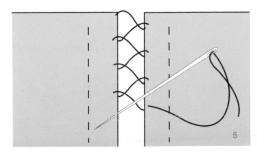

5

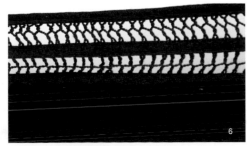

6

Seam finishes > Hand sewing techniques

1 Fur jacket by Julien
Macdonald, A/W08.

'*I love to take things that are everyday and comforting and make them into the most luxurious things in the world.*'

Marc Jacobs

This chapter deals specifically with the range of techniques used for specialist fabrics and materials. Finishes and treatments that are added to a fabric at any stage of its process can make the material difficult to cut, sew or finish. These include felted wools, lace, sequinned and beaded fabrics, knits and fabrics that have a nap, such as velvet. A material such as fur or leather, whether it is real or synthetic, also requires specialist knowledge in its construction.

Felted fabrics

1   An abutted seam.

2   A top-stitched hem finish.

3   A top-stitched hem with
    1cm turned under.

4   A flat fell seam.

5   Calvin Klein dress made of
    felted wool, A/W08.
    Catwalking.com.

Felted woven fabrics are shrunk and compressed with heat, moisture
and friction to produce a dense appearance. Some of the better-
known felted fabrics are loden, melton or fleece. The edges of a
felted fabric do not fray so seams can be left unfinished. It is most
common to use a plain stitched seam with topstitching or a welt
seam for light- to medium-weight felted fabric. But there are many
more techniques to choose from, such as:

Abutted seam

Abutted seams (or channel seams)
can be used as decorative seams,
by applying a ribbon or any contrast
fabric as an under layer.

- Prepare a 3cm strip as an
  under layer and mark the
  centre of the strip. You can
  use contrasting or matching
  fabric.

- Place the raw edge of both
  sides of the garment pieces on
  to the centre line of the strip.
  The strip is lying on the wrong
  side of the fabric pieces with
  the right side up.

- Now top-stitch each side
  of the garment pieces on to
  the strip.

- If required, you can also leave
  a gap to show more of the
  decorative strip.

Topstitched hem

The best way to finish a felted fabric
garment is with a topstitched hem,
but you could also use a blanket
stitch, which creates a certain look
and finishes off the edge.

- Add allowance for a hem.

- Turn the hem allowance to the
  wrong side of the garment.

- Top-stitch the hem down. This
  can be done at any width,
  stitch length and row position
  depending on the design
  choice. Use any type of
  thread (colour or thickness)
  or use decorative stitching.

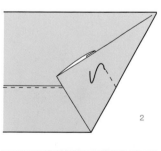

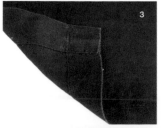

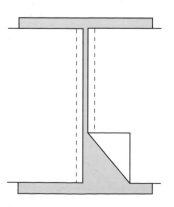

Non-woven flat fell seam

A variation of the flat fell seam is
strong enough for non-woven felted
fabrics.

- Allow 1.5cm for the seam
  allowance.

- Put the wrong sides together
  and sew a straight line.

- Press the seam flat to one
  side.

- From the inner layer trim off
  2–3mm.

- Top-stitch the top layer down
  along the edge.

- To strengthen the seams
  use a fusible web before
  top-stitching.

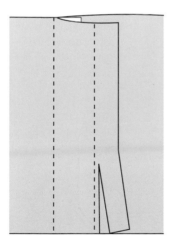

4

5

Lace

1   Christian Lacroix, haute
    couture, S/S08.
    Catwalking.com.

2   Technical drawing showing
    how to cut lace fabric and
    create an appliqué seam.

Lace is a decorative fabric with an open structure. It is made by hand or machine using knitting, braiding, looping and knotting techniques. Lace is used for trimming on lingerie, collars and cuffs or as appliqué, traditionally on bridal or evening wear. It can be fine- to heavyweight, in different fibres such as linen, wool, cotton, polyester or nylon and has more stretch in the width than in the length. Lace is fragile and needs to be handled with care. It is also expensive. You will require more fabric when cutting out because most lace fabrics have a horizontal or vertical pattern that should be matched up, both for garment construction and for trimmings.

1

Appliqué seams

Appliqué seams are used on lace garments to ensure that none of the side or centre back seams are visible.

- Cut the pattern as usual.

- Place the pattern right-side up on to the lace. Lay out the pieces, leaving space between them, aligning the pattern design of the fabric from front side seam to back side seam.

- Be careful with the centre front and centre back when placing the pieces for a central pattern.

- First thread mark the original side seams of the pattern on to the lace fabric.

- Then thread mark the overlapping pattern on to the front panel.

- Cut the overlapping piece (front piece) following the pattern and add some allowance (this can be cut off later).

- Then cut the back piece (this is the corresponding under layer) with a 1cm allowance.

- Put the overlapping layer on top (right-side up) and pin the thread-marked front and back side seam lines together.

- Baste the new side seam and check the fit for small alterations, before sewing the pieces permanently together.

- Appliqué around the lace pattern with a small zigzag stitch, either by hand or with the sewing machine.

- Trim all excess allowances off each layer and press the seams carefully at a low temperature.

Appliquéd lace edging and set-in lace pieces

When integrating lace pieces into a garment or finishing, such as on lace-trimmed necklines or hemlines, great care has to be applied to make the fabric and lace look like a single piece. Lace application should not look like an afterthought, but as though it is part of the fabric.

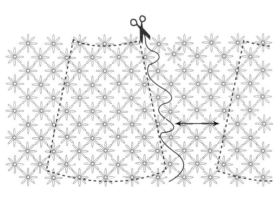

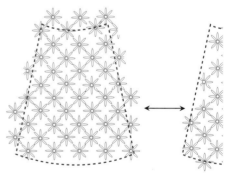

Leather

1 Leather hand-sewing needles and leather machine needles with a wedge point.

2 Welt seam on leather sample.

3 Leather seam with topstitch.

4 Leather seam with tape for reinforcement.

5 Glue and brush to hold down leather seam allowance and hemlines.

6 Leather jacket by D&G, Dolce and Gabbana, S/S08.

Leather is one of the oldest materials used to cover up the human body. It is not a type of fabric but the skin of a mammal or reptile and is therefore sold by the skin and not by the metre. The hair of the skin is removed and the grain revealed by a process called tanning (leather can be tanned using several products including: tannin, chrome, alum or oil). The skin will go through a finishing process after the tanning to apply colour or a different surface, for example shiny or matt. It is called leather when the outside of the skin is tanned and finished and known as suede when the inside is finished.

Sewing leather

1

Leather does not fray and therefore the edges do not have to be finished. When sewing leather use a special leather needle and do not pin the skin as it leaves marks. Also, the garment cannot be let out, as it will show the stitches. Leather is sensitive to heat from the iron and may get stained and creased permanently. When working with suede, watch out for the nap.

2

A leather or suede garment requires a different approach in its construction compared to one made in fabric. To avoid disappointment, always experiment with scraps of leather first, trying out seams and other areas that can cause problems.

- Use a polyester thread (or if the leather is heavy then try a top-stitching thread, which is thicker than a normal stitching thread). Do not use cotton or cotton-wrapped polyester thread as the treatment used on leather or suede will make the thread rot.

- Start by trying a universal machine needle first. If it skips stitches use a leather needle that is wedge pointed.

- Use a Teflon foot, roller or leather foot on the sewing machine. The foot may leave marks on the leather so try first on a scrap of leather.

3

Seams for leather

Always consider the weight and style of garment when choosing the seam type. A plain seam works for all thin- to medium-weight leathers. For the heavier range of leathers use a lapped seam, as it will create less bulk. Other types of seams are the plain leather seam, slot seam, welt seam or for extra stability and reinforcement, the taped seam.

- Instead of ironing the seams, these are pressed down or pounded with a cloth-covered hammer.

- Glue (use leather glue, which is more flexible) or top-stitch the seams down to keep them flat. Skive the edges off the seams to avoid bulk.

- Darts are stitched to the dart point, than slashed open and glued or top-stitched down.

Hems for leather

To achieve a flat hem on curved edges, cut out triangular notches.

- Hemlines can be glued or top-stitched. Pound the hemline first to get a fold line, then glue or top-stitch close to the fold lines. This is especially important when applying a lining so that the hem edge is left free, allowing you to machine stitch the lining to it.

- For heavier leather use the raw edge facing. If the leather is nice inside, why not finish off the hemming by turning the hem inside out (wrong-side-out hem).

Fastenings for leather

Suitable fastenings for leather garments are zips of all kinds and bound, slash-stitched buttonholes or buttons with loops. Hook-and-loop fastenings and lacings can also work well. When sewing on the buttons and hooks use a leather needle and a waxed thread. Apply a small button as a stay button on the facing side.

6

4

5

Fur

1   Fur hat and miniskirt by
Julien Macdonald, A/W08.

Real fur, like leather, comes from an animal but with the hair still attached. All real furs have dense short hairs called 'under fur' and longer, softer hairs called 'guard hairs'. Real fur is very expensive to buy and, because of where it comes from, in many countries is unpopular to wear. However, manufactured imitations are becoming more and more sophisticated. Fake fur fabric is easier to cut as it comes on the metre and not in skins. It is also easier to sew. The quality is so good that it is often mistaken for real fur.

Real fur can be processed to make it softer and it can be bleached, dyed or stencilled to change its colour. It can also be sheared or curled to give it a different texture and look.

Sewing fur

A number of methods can be employed to make working with fur easier.

- Use a polyester thread for real fur and any type of thread for fur fabric, as long as the thread is strong enough.

- For real fur, start by trying a universal machine needle. If it skips stitches use a wedge-pointed leather needle. For woven fur fabrics, a universal machine needle should work well.

- For real fur use a Teflon foot, roller or leather foot on the sewing machine and a standard machine foot for fur fabric.

Tips for working with fur
- Fur has a nap and sometimes looks livelier when cut upside down.

- When cutting real or fake fur, make sure to cut the skin only and not the hair. Mark your pattern pieces on the skin side and slide a razor blade, mat knife or scissors carefully through just the skin.

1

Plain seam

To avoid the fur hair being caught in the seam push the pile towards the garment, then stitch the seam and turn around to the fur side. To release fur pile caught in a seam, use a pin and carefully pull the pile out. Also trim away the pile in the seam allowance to avoid extra bulk.

- Fake fur fabric can be carefully pressed with a low-temperature iron on the wrong side. If seams do not lay flat on a real fur garment then use hand stitching to flatten the seams down.

- The best way to hem a fur garment is to tape it or face it with leather.

- To fasten a fur garment use faced and inseamed buttonholes, leather button loops, covered hooks and eyes or simply wrap the front and close with a leather belt. Zips should only be used on short-haired fur, as long-haired furs will get caught in between the zip teeth.

Knits and stretch-woven fabrics

1   Five-thread overlocked side seam of a t-shirt.

2   Coverstitch with two- and three-needle effects on a hemline.

3   Bound neckline of a t-shirt with coverstitching.

4   A basic skirt block for woven fabrics can be reduced to a jersey skirt block by taking in the skirt to allow for the stretch.

5   The final stretch/jersey skirt block.

6   T-shirt by Courtney McWilliams with a raw edge finish on the neckline.

Linking one or more yarns into a series of interlocking loops makes up a knit fabric. Horizontal rows of knit are known as 'courses' and vertical rows are known as 'wales'. Knitted and stretch-woven fabric is comfortable because of its stretchiness. However, care must be taken when working with these fabrics as pressing and heat can cause the fabric to lose its shape.

Types of knitted and stretch-woven fabric

There are two types of knitted fabric: one is the weft knit, which is one continuous yarn. This is used to produce fabrics such as jersey, ribbing, sweatshirt knits, inter-locks and double knit. The second is the warp knit, which uses many yarns and one stitch (warp) to produce fabric that is flat with straight edges (jersey, on the other hand, is less stable, runs easily and curls at all cut edges). The best-known warp knit is tricot, which is used, for example, in lingerie. Another is the raschel knit, which has a lacy, openwork appearance. Weft and warp knits use only four basic stitches: plain, rib, purl and warp.

Stretch-woven fabrics must have at least 20 per cent stretch in either direction; lengthwise or crosswise. These fabrics can be made with textured yarn, either curled or crimped. They can be given a special finish or woven with yarns made from elastomers (elastomer is a synthetic material that has extensibility and complete elastic recovery). Some well-known stretch fibres are Spandex or Lycra. They can be mixed with cotton, wool or any synthetic fibres. Any traditional fabric such as corduroy, denim, satin or lace can be combined with stretch yarns and therefore gain the characteristic of knits, such as comfort, wrinkle-resistance and a better fit.

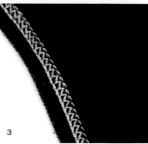

Sewing knitted and stretch-woven fabric

Due to its fragile nature, knitted and stretch-woven fabric requires some specific construction methods.

- Use a polyester or cotton-wrapped polyester, woolly nylon or elasticated thread.

- Try a universal machine needle for stretch-woven fabrics and if it skips, use a ballpoint and/or stretch needle. It may also be worth trying twin needles.

- Seams can be put together using specialist machinery such as the coverstitch or five-thread overlocker, which will allow the stretch-woven fabric or knit to stretch.

- The hem finishing, like the seams, depends on the style of the garment. You can choose from a variety of hand and machine finishings. For example, if you are working by hand use a cross-stitch, which will give the stretch needed in the hemming. If you are working on a machine use a cover-stitch with twin needle effects or a zigzag stitch. Applying a binding or ribbon to finish off the edge works well, or try elastic casing and elastic lace or any other elastic tape. A clean cut raw edge also looks interesting if it does not allow the knit to run.

Tips for working with knits and stretch-woven fabric

- When cutting out, make sure you allow the fabric to relax on the table and don't stretch it at any point of the cutting process. Also use fine pins and very sharp scissors.

- Be careful when pressing stretch-woven fabrics and knits as neither will take a hot iron. When pressing, steam on to the seam and afterwards press down the seam with the fingers.

- Fastenings on knit and stretch-woven fabrics are tricky. Always use an interlining or tapes to restrict the part where the fastening is placed. For example, use a decorative non-stretch tape on the outside or inside of the button stand position. This will keep the garment closed and prevent it from stretching into a different size. Zips, Velcro or magnetic closings can also be used as fastenings.

4 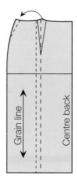 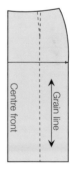 5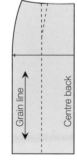

6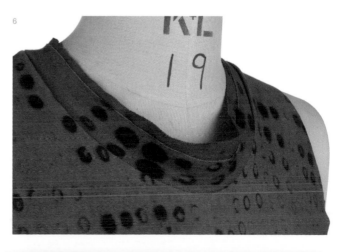

Sequinned and beaded fabrics

Sequinned and beaded fabrics are glamorous and in the past have been used mainly for eveningwear and special occasions. It is now much more common to use these fabrics for daywear. Sequins, beads and other sparkling stones are sewn or glued on to an underlayer of fabric such as chiffon, satin, taffeta or knits.

Sewing sequinned and beaded fabric

These fabrics are not easy to handle and extra time and care needs to be considered when using them.

- Beads and sequins are applied to the fabric with repeated chain stitch. This means that if pulled from one side, it will unravel badly.

- The best thread to use is polyester or cotton-wrapped polyester for both hand and machine sewing.

- Use a universal machine needle and a hand-sewing beading needle. When using the sewing machine tack the stitch size down to 2.5mm.

- If required, you can also leave a gap to show more of the decorative strip.

Tips for working with sequinned and beaded fabric

- Sequinned fabrics can be uncomfortable on bare skin, therefore the garment should be lined.

- Some sequinned and beaded fabrics can have a pattern and will therefore need matching up. The fabrics usually have a nap/direction and should be cut from a single layer. Make sure to use old but sharp scissors as the fabric dulls scissor blades.

- Avoid darts and add flare through slash and spread rather than gathers and pleats. Simple sleeve solutions like the kimono or raglan show off the fabric better than a set-in sleeve. Try not to break up the fabric design unnecessarily.

- Before purchasing a sequinned fabric check the width, because most are very narrow (114cm/45in).

Assembling sequinned and beaded fabric garments

These fabrics are used to their best advantage by employing a simple style with a minimum of seams.

- The seams to use are a plain seam; a double-stitched seam (two close rows of straight stitch lines); a hairline seam (two close rows of straight stitch and zigzag stitch lines) or you can used a taped seam for reinforcement.

- When the garment pieces are cut, take away the sequins along the seams. Only sew the underlayer of fabric together, do not sew through sequins.

- Once the seams are closed add the missing sequins along the seam line by hand (this will make the seam disappear) and also secure the loose ones around the seam. The same procedure should be used with a beaded fabric.

- Facing and hemming can be done by using tapes, bands, bindings, ribbing or any fabric/lining facings.

- Another way of finishing hemlines is to superlock the edges. Superlock is a very fine and tight overlocking stitch.

- Depending on the style of garment use a light zip, hook and eye or loops and buttons to fasten.

1   Sequinned trouser by Alexander McQueen, A/W08. Catwalking.com.

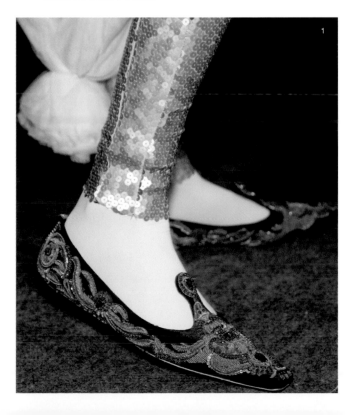

1

Velvet

Napped or pile fabrics go through a process called 'napping', whereby fibre ends are raised to the surface to be either clipped, brushed flat or left standing up. This process can be applied on one or both sides of woven or knitted fabrics.

Pile fabrics are woven with an extra set of yarn. Velvet is a popular fabric of the napped or pile family. Originally velvet was made from silk yarns. Today velvets range from light- to heavyweight and can be woven from cotton, rayon or polyester. Velvet has an extra set of warp yarns and is woven as two layers of fabric. The pile, which joins the layers together, is cut after the fabric is woven. The result is a much denser pile, giving the fabric a rich texture.

Sewing velvet

Care needs to be taken with velvet once it has been cut as the pile frays badly at its raw edges. Ironing and pressing velvet can also damage the fabric by flattening the pile so try to press on the inside of the garment or use a velvet board to avoid using too much pressure. Some other tips for sewing velvet include:

- Use a universal machine needle and take the pressure off the sewing foot. Try using a roller or even-feed machine foot or a zipper foot.

- When sewing seams, make sure you hand tack the seams together as velvet creeps badly and sometimes puckers during the sewing process. You can use a plain seam or tape your seams for extra stability.

- Hemming can be sewn by hand with blind hemstitching or faced with a lighter fabric by machine.

- Clean up frayed edges on seams by binding or overlocking the seam allowance.

1

Transparent fabrics

Beautiful transparent fabrics range from crisp to soft and light- to heavyweight. The best-known crisp, semi-transparent to transparent fabrics are organza and organdie made from silk, cotton or synthetics, as well as marquisette and handkerchief linen. These types of fabrics are easier to cut and sew then the soft transparent ones. The most common types of soft, semi-transparent and transparent fabrics are chiffon, georgette and crepe chiffon. These fabrics are so lightweight they are tricky to cut and difficult to sew. You will also find fabrics that you can categorise in between crisp and soft such as voile, batiste, shirtings or gauze. These fabrics might be difficult to work with but are worth all the effort, as they are stunning to look at and delightful to wear.

Sewing transparent fabrics

It is worth noting that the softer the fabric, the more time and space you will need to work with it.

- Use a fine (60–70) universal machine needle and reduce the stitch length to 1.25–2mm, which is a very small stitch.

- Match the thread to the fabric and use a fine to extra fine polyester thread or mercerised cotton.

- Iron all the creases out of the fabric with a dry iron.

- Pin the fabric carefully on to a piece of thin paper the same size as the fabric. The paper is supposed to stop the fabric from moving around, as it is famously slippery.

- After securing the fabric to the paper, add a third layer of paper with the pattern pieces copied on to it. Pin all three layers together and cut out with sharp scissors.

- Make sure that all marks within the pattern piece are thread marked (use a fine needle and extra fine thread). Do not use chalk marks, which will show permanently on the good side of the fabric.

- Carefully clean up the inside of the garment, as the transparent fabric shows all kinds of hems, seams and facings on the outside of the garment. There are several methods you can use for the seams, for example French seams or bindings. The best method for hemming a chiffon garment is a pin-hem and if you work on a budget use a superlock as a finishing. Slip-stitch is a nice hand sewing stitch for hem or edge finishings.

- When it comes to pressing the fabric, consider the material and always try first on a scrap piece. Sometimes using a dry iron makes the fabric static. If this happens, use an antistatic spray.

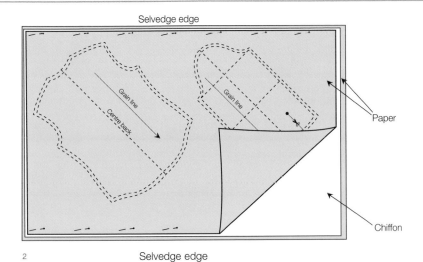

Selvedge edge

Grain line

Grain line

Centre back

Paper

Chiffon

2

Selvedge edge

3

1   Chiffon dress by Yuki with French seam finish and a pin hem.

2   Example of a layout for cutting fine fabrics.

3   Example of a pin hem finish on a sleeve hemline.

4   Sample of a superlock finish.

5   Close-up of the French seam finish on the dress by Yuki.

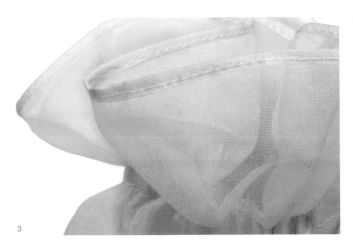

4

5

1   Backstage image at Christophe Josse's haute couture A/W06 show. Catwalking.com.

'*I created flower women with gentle shoulders and generous bosoms, with tiny waists like stems and skirts belling out like petals.*'

Christian Dior

At the top of the garment manufacturing chain are haute couture and the tailoring crafts, which involve working with individual customers. The garments are constructed using traditional methods such as hand sewing and intricate cuts. The fabric and finishing can often heavily influence the designing process and the designs will often work to ensure that they are displayed to their best advantage on the body.

A lot of time, consideration and energy is put into a couture or tailored garment. The result is a garment that fits flawlessly, using the finest luxury fabrics, put together with skillful hands by dressmakers and tailors who are proud of their work and the name they work for. To be working as a tailor on Savile Row, for example, or in an atelier for an haute couture house conveys the feeling of exclusivity through history and tradition.

Haute couture

1 *Monsieur Dior et nous (1947–1957),* Esmeralda de Réthy and Jean-Louis Perreau, Anthese (1999).

2 Fitting of a dress by Dior.

1

Translated literally from French into English, the phrase 'haute couture' means 'sewing at a high level'. Couturiers use only the finest and most luxurious fabrics. Sometimes these have been custom made. A couture garment is meant to fit flawlessly as a result of many fittings and will include perfectly designed proportions for the individual client. Adjustments are made on garments to balance the body shape of the customer. These can include changes to the collar, the proportions of the pockets (one can be slightly bigger than the other), shoulder seams (one can be narrower than the other), or padding in one shoulder to make it higher than the other. For a full figure all horizontal seam lines are adjusted, not just the waist and hemline. This attention to detail is the essence of haute couture. With the help of the toile, every design detail is planned so that any motifs, stripes or checks are matched and positioned to the best advantage for the client's figure. At garment openings a motif will match so perfectly you have to look twice to discover the fastening. On suits and two-piece designs the fabric pattern continues uninterrupted from neck to hem.

2

The history

The origins of haute couture lie in the eighteenth century, with many attributing its birth to the couturier, Rose Bertin (the milliner to Marie Antoinette) and Charles Frederick Worth. Prior to this, clothing would have been made by the couturier to the specifications of the customer. It was not until the mid-nineteenth century that Charles Frederick Worth, who was originally from England, first introduced his customers to garments made up from his own ideas. He showed his collection of finished designs on live models – a novel exercise at the time. He achieved colossal success and opened up a new direction in fashion. Once the customer had selected an outfit from the portfolio (today called a look-book) and specified the colour and fabric, the outfit would be made to measure in the atelier (workshop). This is still common practice.

In France, haute couture is a protected name and can only be used by companies that work to a certain standard, as defined by the 'Chambre de commerce et d'industrie de Paris'. The rules that define those design houses allowed to become an haute couture label were established in 1945 but have since been updated. To become a member of the 'Chambre syndicale de la haute couture' and to be able to use the term 'haute couture' in its label and advertising or in any other way, a design house must follow three main regulations: to provide an atelier in Paris that employs at least 15 people full-time; to present a collection with at least 35 outfits including day- and eveningwear to the Paris press; and to provide a service to private clients with bespoke designed garments.

Across Europe the term couture has been used loosely to describe tailor-made and high fashion garments, which can lead to confusion for customers. A collection of garments produced more than once and to a size range is called prêt-à-porter, the French term for 'ready to wear'. As they struggle with their vast costs, these days couture houses also produce prêt-a-porter collections. The purpose of a couture show is to enhance the prestige of the house.

In 1946 there were 106 official haute couture houses. Over the course of the twentieth century this number dropped dramatically to 18 and today there may be as few as ten: Adeline Andre, Chanel, Christian Lacroix, Dior, Dominique Sirop, Emanuel Ungaro, Frank Sorbier, Givenchy, Jean Paul Gaultier and Jean Louis Scherrer. There are also three correspondent or foreign member houses: Elie Saab, Giorgio Armani and Valentino.

Designing haute couture

1   *Paul Poiret fashion memoir*, Francois Baudot, Thames and Hudson (1997). Sketch of an evening cloak by Georges Lepape (1911) and a dressing gown with a pattern designed by Dufy (1923).

2   *Balenciaga fashion memoir*, Marie-Andree Jouve, Thames and Hudson (1997). Black coat with white mink cape (1967) and 'Four-sided' cocktail dress.

3   *Charles James fashion memoir*, Richard Martin, Thames and Hudson (1997). James's 'Four-leaf Clover' evening dress (1953) and a drawing of the inside by Bill Wilkinson (1982).

The construction of a couture garment may look effortless, but it takes many hours to produce that effortless look. Equipped with a thorough understanding of the human body and knowledge of fibres and fabrics, the couturier may begin with either the fabric or the silhouette.

When the fabric arrives the couturier drapes unfolded lengths of each fabric over a mannequin or a house model to see how the material hangs on the lengthwise-, cross- and bias-grain lines. Using this information as a guide he or she starts the design process by drawing sketches for the collection. The design sketches are distributed to the atelier. Depending on the type of garment, the sketches will go to the tailoring workroom (*atelier de tailleur*) or the dressmaking workroom (*atelier de flou*). Then the appropriate weight of muslin/calico is selected and the toile is draped on the mannequins to duplicate the design sketch. This drape provides the basic pattern from which the garment will be sewn.

The toile will be made with all the necessary underpinnings and put together with the same care as the final garment. This toile is then fitted on the house model and reworked. Sometimes toiles are made in the final fabric straight away, allowing the couturier to appreciate the garment to its full potential.

Once the toile is approved it is carefully taken apart and pressed so that it can serve as a pattern. After the fabric is cut and thread marked the prototype is ready to be fitted on the house model once again. This process will be repeated until the designer is satisfied. Finally, accessories are selected by the couturier for the press show and the design is entered in the *Livre de fabrication* (production or look-book).

1

Paul Poiret (1879–1947)
Poiret changed fashion by creating a new silhouette. The cut of his dresses were clean and uncomplicated in contrast to the other dresses worn at the turn of the century. He was inspired by the orient and exoticism. Paul Poiret was also the first to build a virtual fashion empire.

2

Balenciaga (1895–1972)
Cristobel Balenciaga's work has a strictly modern appeal. He was a master of the refined, tailored garment that skimmed the body contours. He made the wearer seem taller by pitching the waistline just above the natural waist. He created some of the most powerful styles in the twentieth century and was often called the designers' designer.

3

Charles James (1906–1978)
Charles James invented the American haute couture. He created an ideal of female beauty with his magnificent sculptured dresses. James was a perfectionist who combined the science of design with the eroticism of fashion. Influenced by nature, he named his designs after living things such as the 'Petal' or the famous 'Four-leaf Clover' evening dress.

Haute couture > **Designing haute couture** > Tailoring

Tailoring

1 Yves Saint Laurent,
   Backstage, A/W08.
   Catwalking.com.

2 Hardy Amies opened on
   Savile Row in 1946.

3 Typical men's outfit of 1833.

4 Typical men's outfit of 1931.

The term 'tailoring' refers not only to specific hand and machine sewing, and pressing techniques but also to a garment whose form and contours are not influenced solely by the wearer's body shape. A tailor has the knowledge to keep the structure of a jacket design in place and improve the appearance of the wearer's natural shape. They might, for example, use different materials to underlay and pad the shoulder and chest areas with great precision.

1

A history of tailoring

It is generally agreed that the accepted style in menswear in the early nineteenth century has remained recognisably similar to the present day. There has naturally been some re-proportioning of length and silhouette, either more defined or looser, but the components of a tailored suit – the coat, vest and trouser – have a direct line of descent from the end of the Napoleonic wars.

What is most surprising is that the colour palette of these early years has remained virtually unchanged. The use of dark, neutrally coloured wool juxtaposed with white linen or cotton reflected a new mood in society. A growing awareness of the importance of hygiene made the wearing of fresh linen an obvious demonstration that cleanliness was indeed next to godliness. George 'Beau' Brummell, 1778–1840, an early practitioner of this new concept of dress, was fastidious in his cleanliness, discarding several cravats at one dressing as not being suitably washed, pressed and finished. He awakened a more general interest in neat dressing and gave a great example of a well-dressed man himself.

Since the first tailor's establishment opened in 1785, London's Savile Row has become world renowned for custom-tailored suiting (also called 'bespoke' tailoring, because cloth reserved for a customer was 'spoken for' by him).

In 1969, Tommy Nutter and Edward Sexton opened their shop Nutters. They pioneered shop window display and revolutionised Savile Row. Today, Ozwald Boateng, Richard James and Timothy Everest are among a new wave of master tailors who cater for those requiring a perfectly fitted suit of outstanding quality and craftsmanship.

Tailoring is a time-honoured skill that is complex and specialised in its technical knowledge. Many professionals in the fashion industry worship the tailor's craft and would not attempt to undertake tailored apparel. Organised in guilds and brotherhoods, the tailoring trade has been protected by the people working in it, who pass on and safeguard knowledge very carefully.

Over time, new machinery and fusing materials have been introduced to the tailor's market. However, many are not convinced and prefer to use only hand sewing methods to ensure the precise shaping of the fabric. A sewing machine is only used to close up seams and darts.

Today, tailoring can be split into two categories: traditional custom-tailors who continue to practise their craft more or less as it was a century ago, and industrial tailors, who use speedier and therefore less expensive alternative and construct their jackets and coats to an industrial tailored finish. This means that the chest pieces, pockets, collar and shoulders are reinforced by an iron-on interlining and prefabricated pieces. Pad stitching (pad stitch is used to join two layers of materials together using a diagonal stitch which is staggered from one row to the next) is replaced by a machine stitch that replicates the stitching pattern. The shoulder roll is machine stitched into the sleeve head instead of being hand sewn and can therefore be carefully placed to the individual requirements of the customer. The industrial tailored suit can be manufactured to a very high standard, but will never deliver the individual fit and exclusive feel of a custom-tailored suit.

2

3

4

Tailoring techniques

1   An inside-out tailored jacket showing the under structure.

2   Woollen fabric and lining sample booklet, published by 2000 Tailoring Ltd. London.

3   Tailored jacket with basting stitching in working progress.

A lot of components play a significant role in creating an excellently fitted tailored garment, from the right choice of fabric and the shape and design of the garments, to the skilled measuring of the body and the specific techniques employed.

This section will introduce you to some of the materials and techniques used by tailors for constructing jackets.

1

2

The understructure

This is made from different kinds of canvas and interfacing, soft cotton flannel, cotton twill tape, strips of cotton or lambswool, Melton for the collar stand, pocketing fabric and strong, lightweight lining.

The fabrics

Woollen fabric used for tailored suits can fall into two categories: worsteds and woollens. Worsted fabric is woven from long, finely combed wool. It is a firm fabric with a flat surface, ideal for traditional tailored business suits. Woollen fabrics are woven from shorter, uncombed wool fibres. These fibres are loosely twisted and woven much less tightly than the worsteds. The effect is a soft, easy fabric, such as a Harris Tweed. Other fabrics can also be used, such as silk and linen.

Tweed
A woollen fabric named after the river Tweed, which flows through the Scottish Borders textile areas. Harris Tweed is one variation, made from pure virgin wool that is dyed and spun in Harris (in the Outer Hebrides) and hand woven by the islanders in their homes.

The hand stitches

The following stitches are commonly used in tailoring:

Basting stitch attaches two or more pieces of fabric temporarily. It is also used to make construction and placement lines.

Pad stitching is used to attach the sew-in interfacing and to shape the garment at the same time.

Slip-stitch attaches the lining edge to the hem invisibly as well as the edges of pockets to the garment.

Fell stitching holds the stay tape (a narrow fabric tape) in place.

Cross-stitch invisibly secures interfacing edges to the garment.

Hemstitching invisibly attaches the hem allowance to the garment.

Tailor's tacks are used to mark fabrics, for example on the folding line of the lapel rolling line or pocket placement.

3

Trimming, notching and grading

All edges in a tailored garment should be flat and sharp without noticeable bulk. Seam edges, collar tips and pocket flaps should roll slightly to the inside, towards the body. To avoid bulky seams use the following methods:

Trimming. Trim sewn-in interfacings close to the seam lines. The seam allowance of the collar, lapel and bagged-out pocket points can also be trimmed.

Notching. Notch the seam allowance by taking out wedges at the outside curves. On a deep curve bring notches closer together than on a shallow one. Always notch close to the stitching line!

Grading. Trim the seam allowance back in a staggered fashion whereby the widest seam allowance is layered towards the garment's right side. This is done to cushion the remaining seams, so they do not show through to the right side.

The pressing techniques

Darts and seams create shape in a piece of fabric. It is best, therefore, to use a tailor's ham or a rounded pressing board to maintain the shape. Press the vertical darts towards centre front or centre back. If using a thick fabric, cut open the dart and press flat. To get a nice, flat point at the dart end use a needle and insert right to the point. Press with the needle in place and remove it afterwards.

To avoid over pressing, which causes the imprint of seams, edges and darts to appear on the outside, use paper strips or pieces of the same kind of fabric to underlay the seam allowance and edges.

Moulding is the stretching and shrinking of fabric to fit the body shape. The best fabric to use is wool, which takes on the new shape and holds it as if it had always been

that way. A tailor would reshape the two-piece sleeve to accentuate the forward bend in the elbow area. The trouser leg would be reshaped before a seam allowance is attached. For example, the back panel on the inside leg is stretched at the top to fit on to the front panel, thus achieving a closer fit to the bottom and crotch area.

The taping

On a jacket certain areas need to be taped with cotton twill tape. This avoids stretching during construction and strengthens the edges to prevent the jacket losing its shape when worn.

The areas to tape are:
neckline
armhole
the fold in the lapel
the edges of the lapel all the way down to the hemline (some tailors continue along the edge of the front hemline)

When taping an edge, take the measurement from the pattern for the tape length. You will find that the fabric edge has already stretched a bit and that you have to ease the fabric on to the tape.

1

1   Inside the front piece of a jacket showing the taped folding line and taped edges of the lapel.

2   Student's research book on tailoring showing a 'peaked lapel'.

3   Student's research on a tailored collar.

4   Hugo Boss, S/S08, tailored jacket with a welt pocket (chest position) and jetted pocket with flap (hip position).

5   Single-breasted jacket closing with one button.

6   Double-breasted jacket with six buttons, fastening at the second button.

7   Vent with button and buttonhole fastening

8   A keyhole buttonhole.

The collar and lapel

Collars and lapels can change shape with fashion or can keep a traditional look. The line where collar and lapel meet is called a gorge line.

There are different shapes of lapel used in tailoring:
cloverleaf lapel
fish mouth lapel
L-shaped lapel
notched lapel
peaked lapel
shawl collar

2

3

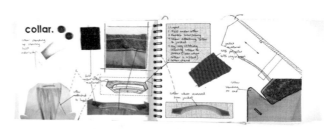

collar.

The pocket shapes

The most popular pocket shapes are:
welt pocket
jetted pocket/piping pocket
jetted pocket/piping pocket with flap
patch pocket
lining/inside pocket

The fastenings

The placement of buttons is crucial, always place a button half an inch below the natural waistline.

A hand-sewn keyhole buttonhole with inserted gimp is the tailor's choice of fastening on a jacket.

Single-breasted jackets should have one or three buttons; double-breasted jackets should have four or six buttons, fastened at the second or third.

Sleeve fastenings are traditionally vents, with a button and buttonhole, which sit at the back of the sleeve. The vent can also be opened with a zip, or without any fastenings at all.

4

5

6

1 Backstage image at
Boudicca's couture S/S08
show. Catwalking.com.

'*It's more like engineering than anything else. It's finding
the limits of what you can do when wrapping the body in
fabric. Everything evolves. Nothing is strictly defined.*'

John Galliano

Draping is modelling or shaping a piece of fabric on a
mannequin (also called a model-stand, dress form or dummy)
or a life model. Madeleine Vionnet (in the 1920s) and Madame
Alix Gres (1930s) were the first couture designers to devote
their talent and time to the art of draping. To this day, designers
look back on their achievements and recreate
their techniques.

For the designer who is looking for a more exciting cut and
who is prepared for the unexpected, draping is an excellent
way of approaching design and pattern development. Let
yourself be inspired by the texture, colour and fall of the
fabric and see the design evolve before your eyes.

Marker pen (1)
To mark permanent lines on the garment.

Scissors and shears (2)
Good quality scissors are important. You will need a small pair of scissors (approximately 8–14cm) for trimming and notching the fabric and a larger pair of shears (approximately 14–20cm) to reshape the fabric.

Tailor's chalk (3)
To mark temporary lines on the garment.

Camera (4)
It is very useful to have a camera to hand to document all the stages, especially the end result of each drape. To recreate a drape without any points of reference is time-consuming and often leads to disappointment.

Fine pins (5)
Use sharp, fine, non-rusting pins to fix the fabric pieces together and to anchor the fabric to the mannequin.

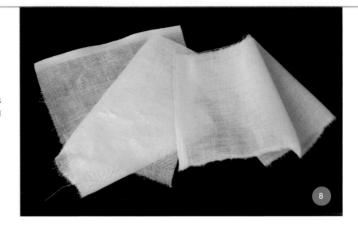

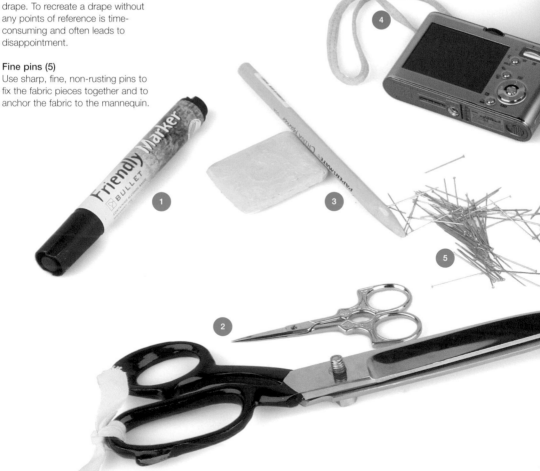

Modelling tools and equipment

There is a vast range of mannequins available. It is vital before starting with the drape to have a close look at the model stand you are working on. Take measurements and analyse the general shape of the stand to work out if it covers the look and size you are after. In addition, you should have the following tools and equipment to hand before starting to drape.

Tape measure (6)
Use a 150cm/60in tape measure.

Style tape (7)
Use a narrow (fabric or sticky) tape to mark style lines as well as the bust-, waist- and hiplines.

Material for draping (8)
The best option is to drape in the final fabric, but this is also the most expensive way. The next best thing is to drape with a material closest in weight, fall and texture to the final fabric. Popular choices are calico, muslin or jersey. These fabrics are inexpensive and the grain line is easy to recognise. Knitwear and jersey garments should always be draped in fabric of a similar character, for example inexpensive knit or jersey.

Grain line and draping

1   Length grain.

2   Cross grain.

3   Bias grain.

4   Mannequin with drape and
     marked information on
     drape.

The direction of the grain line will strongly affect how the fabric hangs on the body. The grain line can be used in three different ways.

You can start draping the fabric on to the mannequin using the straight grain/lengthwise grain (warp), which runs parallel to the selvedge. This grain line can be used if you want to work close to the body or for garment styles that do not require any stretch.

When using the crosswise grain (weft), hold the fabric on to the mannequin so that the selvedge runs parallel to the bust-, waist- or hiplines. The fabric has a little more give/stretch used on the cross than with the straight grain. Fabric on the cross might be used for wider pieces or because of the fabric's pattern/motif or shine.

To gain shape without darts and achieve beautiful soft drapes, use a bias grain. Fold one corner of the fabric in a diagonal to the selvedge, creating a 45-degree fold line. This fold line is the true bias.

Experimenting with all three grain lines to start with will give you a good idea about the fall of a fabric. Also take the time to drape different kinds of fabric, such as woven fabrics and jerseys, on to the mannequin and you will instantly see the difference in the draping effect. It is essential to understand the qualities of certain fabrics to be able to use them in the right way and therefore to master the art of draping. A little passion goes a long way.

1

GRAIN LINE

2

GRAIN LINE

3

GRAIN LINE

A balanced pattern

Balancing the pattern of a draped garment ensures that the garment will sit comfortably on the body without swinging to the front, back or either side. Therefore, the side seam of a garment will hang straight up and down and lie correctly on the body. A good way to maintain the balance is by keeping the centre front and centre back on a perfect grain, using the length grain running from top to bottom and the cross grain aligned with the bust line. To sustain a correct balance between the front and back, make sure that the straight grain and the cross grain are positioned at an angle to the side seam.

Before you take your drape off the mannequin, make sure that you mark all information on to the garment, such as centre front and back, side seam position, bustline, waistline hipline and so on.

4

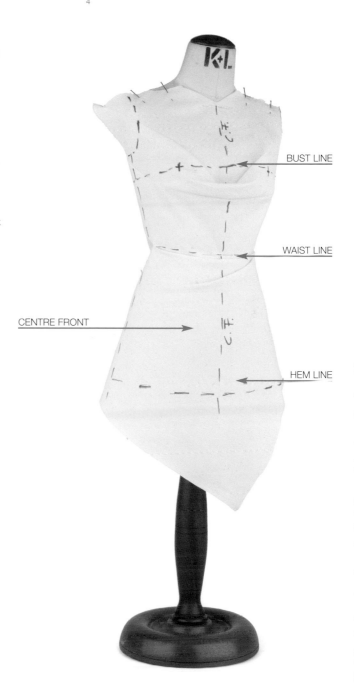

BUST LINE

WAIST LINE

CENTRE FRONT

HEM LINE

Draping style

1   Body contour method
     developed by Tim Williams,
     shown on the mannequin.

2/3 Transferring the pattern to
     paper.

Garments can be draped on to the mannequin, close to the body contour or as an actual shape, structured away from the body. Another approach is loose draping whereby the fabric is anchored on certain parts of the body, such as the shoulder. The fabric hangs loose and drapes fluently from these points.

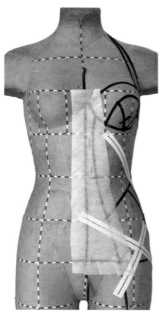

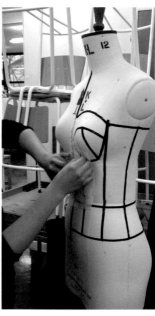

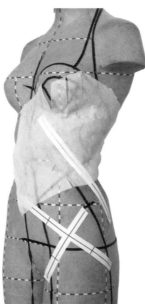

Body contour

During the late 1990s Tim Williams originated lingerie and swimwear for, amongst others, Agent Provocateur and Luella Bartley. He developed a method that enabled him to 'draw' the seams and edges on the mannequin and from this, to quickly and accurately create a pattern. Here he explains his body contour technique:

'For the body contour method you are essentially using the dress stand as your basic block. The method very accurately follows the silhouette of the dummy you are using, making contours around the body to enable a close fitting shape that is then created by the seams. I have used this method on body suits for the film industry, lingerie, swimwear and sportswear. I like working this way because you are 'drawing' your seams and working in three dimensions from the start.

After you have generated a pattern that fits the stand, you then use pattern manipulation techniques to grade the pattern up and down

and increase or decrease any particular parts of the pattern. Remember that creating a pattern to fit a dummy is relatively easy. The next stage, fitting to a person and ensuring comfort and movement, is the most critical application of this technique.

When teaching this method I always ask the students to make up a sample toile as early as possible from the first pattern so that they can give themselves feedback on how the dummy shape relates to their model's shape.

The equipment needed is primarily your dress stand. If you wish, you can use a shop window stand (symmetrical ones only) but you must first cover it in a tight stretch jersey to enable you to place pins. You will also use a selection of coloured biros, some paper, non-woven interfacing and black 6mm stay tape.

The principle is simple: you mark on the stand where the seams will generate the shape. Like drawing,

this simple process relies on the skill of knowing where to place the lines, aesthetically as well as technically.

Always approach this method with a clear idea of what you want in terms of design. Use a swatch of the final fabric so that you can lay it on the surface of the dummy to check how much shaping you need to make. For example, a very rigid fabric with little or no stretch will need a lot of seams or darts to follow the contour of the dummy/body. A stretch jersey, with Lycra for recovery, will form over the body more and so will need fewer seams to allow shape on the garment.'

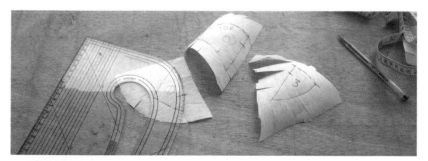

2

3

Loose draping

1   Loosely draped t-shirt by Alexander McQueen, S/S05. Catwalking.com.

2/3   Research work and calico sample of a corset dress by Edina Ozary.

The other method for draping on the stand is loose draping. Lengths of muslin draped loosely on a mannequin create shapes by the fall of the fabric. Some loose drapes use an understructure, for instance a corset to which the drape can be attached.

All loosely draped garments need an anchor point, such as the neckline, shoulder, armhole, bust, waist or hip, from which the fabric will drape. It is important to get the grain line just right, as it influences the drape of the fabric.

1

2

3

Draping tips

- Always use a fabric closest in weight, texture and quality to the final fabric.

- The selvedge is woven more firmly then the rest of the fabric, therefore snip in to the selvedge to release the tension or cut it off completely.

- Always iron the fabric before starting the drape, as the fabric might shrink.

- Watch the grain line; always use the same grain line you intend to use in the final garment.

- Make sure you use fine pins that slide into the mannequin easily.

- Use a mannequin of the right size and shape.

- Consider shoulder pads or padding out certain parts if necessary before starting the drape.

- Do not be worried about cutting into the fabric, it can be replaced or pinned together if cut too deep.

- Understand what makes a garment look old-fashioned or modern. These days a more modern look is achieved by, for example, lowering the waist or shortening the shoulder length.

- Always keep in mind the specific style, proportion and detail you are working towards.

- Get the shell right first and then concentrate on the details.

- When draping an asymmetric garment, only drape one side from centre front to centre back, then later on double the pattern over centre front and centre back.

- Avoid stretching the fabric onto the mannequin, be light handed.

- Always step away from your work and look at it from a distance or move it in front of a mirror and look at it in reflection.

- Drape for an hour and if it does not work to your satisfaction step away and approach the drape later after a break.

Geometric shapes

1

Using simple geometric shapes can be an exciting way of designing on the mannequin. Cut different sized shapes from circles to squares. They can be draped on their own or stitched together for a different result. Try it out; here are some examples pinned to a mannequin.

1   A skirt constructed from a square.

2   Circle pattern with armholes.

3   Triangle and rectangle pattern cut on the bias.

4   A pattern of two triangles and one strip of rectangle cut on the bias.

2

3

4

Books to explore
Some designers like to start
their ideas with a simple
shape and then build upon it.
A lot of well-known designers
now work with geometrical
shapes and so did many of
their famous predecessors.
Here are some book ideas
for you to explore.

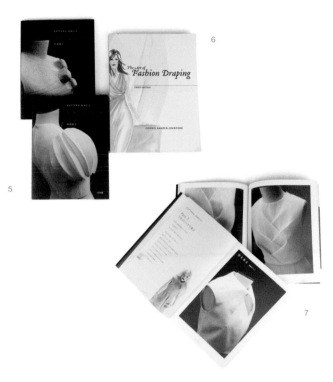

5

6

5   Two versions of *Pattern
     Magic*, Nakamichi Tomoko,
     Vol.1 (2005) and Vol.2 (2007).

6   *The Art of Fashion Draping*,
     Connie Amaden-Crawford,
     Fairchild Books (2005).

7   A taster of *Pattern Magic*.

8   From left to right: *Pierre
     Cardin: Fifty Years of
     Fashion and Design*,
     Elisabeth Langle, Thames
     and Hudson (2005); *Roberto
     Capucci al teatro farnese*,
     Roberto Capucci, Progretti
     museali (1996); *Yeohlee:
     Work Material Architecture*,
     John S. Major and Yeohlee
     Teng, Peleus Press (2003).

9   Image from *Yeohlee: Work
     Material Architecture*.

7

8

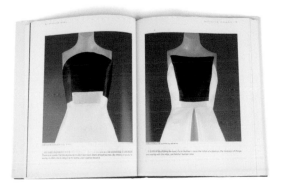

9

Inspired designers

1   Top by Peter Pilotto, A/W08.

2   Detail of a top by Peter
     Pilotto, A/W08.

3   Dress by Peter Pilotto,
     A/W08.

Peter Pilotto and Christopher De
Vos are the designers behind the
Peter Pilotto label.

Pilotto was born in 1977 in Austria
and De Vos was born in 1980 in
Libya. The design duo met while
studying at the Royal Academy of
Fine Arts in Antwerp, Belgium.

**How much designing do you do
by using a 3D approach?**

*Actually very much. We always make
sketches first, of how the lines
should run, but the most important
part happens on the doll and during
the numerous fittings.*

**How important is pattern cutting
and garment construction in the
way you design?**

*Pattern cutting is very important for
our design. We work a lot with print
and it is part of our signature.
However the printed pieces have
interesting pattern constructions
too. Both support each other.*

**How much of your time is spent
on the garment development?**

*In terms of the proportion of time
spent on development and designing
on paper then I would say 85%
actual pattern/garment development
and 15% illustration of those designs
on paper.*

1

2

3

Inspired designers

1   Robert James Curry was designer for the London label Unobilie, along with Kimino Homma, between 2003 and 2006. These experimental shapes are by Unobilie. Robert has since left London and is now working as a lecturer in San Francisco.

Robert James Curry, lecturer in three-dimensional design at the Academy of Art, University of San Francisco.

How much designing do you do by using a 3D approach?

The starting point to everything I do is three dimensional. I never felt comfortable with the approach of drawing a design and then making that design. The basis of everything I work on is the analysis of form – ideas of proportion, the hanging of the cloth, seam placement and volume. Often, the starting point is an idea of geometry, which I cut in fabric using various scales and proportions. It is the resultant form of the connection of two or more planes that is then taken to the mannequin, draped and moulded in various positions and photographed from the relevant angles as the form works on the mannequin. Each different placement can suggest various forms worth pursuing and developing. These various placements can suggest either an entire silhouette or a specific area of interest. It's always about the observation and analysis of the relationship of the fabric to the body.

How important is pattern cutting and garment construction in the way you design?

In one sense, it's everything. Form is the basis of my enquiry. I'm not big on print, texture or embellishment (beading and embroidery). I tend towards a fairly monastic colour palette too. For me the thrill of the whole design process is in the development of the pattern and toile. I'm a great believer in the idea of having to destroy in order to create, so once I have the first toile, it gets cut into, pieces added, fabric taken

away and seams shifted into new positions, added or taken away. Then it's on to the next toile. Once the design is resolved, then the whole concern of construction is addressed. What kind of seam finish works best for the fabric, how will it be lined, cleaned and finished?

How much of your time is spent on garment development?

It is the main element in my work and therefore takes the most time. I must say that I enjoy the initial process of playing with multiple ideas of form, sewn in whatever fabric and moulded on the mannequin in as many ways as possible. I take hundreds of photographs, then go through them and start to edit. Because I don't draw at any stage, I always say that this is my way of sketching ideas. I can come up with multiple design ideas, using scissors and pins, so much quicker than someone sketching with a pencil. You see the garment (or a section of it) appear in front of you in three dimensions. Also, you're creating the pattern, or the basis of it, as you build the design. The moulded form is then marked up and taken apart to be traced on to paper.

1

> *'The dress must follow the body of a woman, not the body following the shape of the dress.'*

Hubert de Givenchy

This chapter offers a brief overview of the history of structured garments and introduces you to the materials and techniques that can be used to achieve support.

Naturally a fabric will always hang downwards and, depending on the weight, thickness, sheerness, drape and stretch, will align to the body shape. In order to obtain a certain structured look it is necessary to provide support through other materials and techniques. Over the years many designers have complemented or deformed the body shape with the use of clever cutting and structured foundations.

To get the right structure under a garment is one of the most challenging, but most enjoyable, aspects of garment construction. It is important to look into the historical development of dress underpinnings and tailored foundations. There is a lot to learn from the old masters and it is up to the creative people of today to use their legacy to help create today's and tomorrow's fashion.

History of supported and structured garments

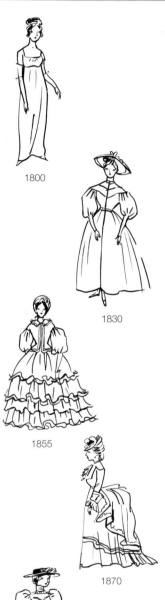

1800

1830

1855

1870

1895

Throughout history, dressmakers and tailors have been working hard to achieve a certain body shape in fashion. Since humans first began to cover their bodies, supportive and structured garments have been used and modified. At first these garments would have been purely for shelter and protection. As time went on however, clothing began to be associated with social and/or economic status and the interest in structured garments that would accentuate certain parts of the body grew and grew.

By 1860 Britain was approaching the peak of its prosperity as the most highly industrialised nation of the world and between the 1860s and the 1880s the Victorian woman's dress was at its most complex. Dresses were supported with increasingly heavy boned corsetry, two or three petticoats, hoops and a bustle.

The crinoline (a stiff petticoat or skirt structure) was out of fashion by 1865 and replaced by a more substantial bustle. This was solidly built from horse hair, steel bones and calico.

The social roles of men and women were distinct and the nineteenth-century female was constrained in her lifestyle choices – she was a dutiful wife or daughter. She was assumed to be weak, fragile and light-headed, something that was not difficult to achieve, as the heavy boned corset would physically weaken women. It was considered bad taste for women not to wear a corset and therefore they would persist in wearing tightly laced corsets, sometimes to such an extent that they could not breathe properly.

By the end of the nineteenth century fashion changed and simple lines began to be regarded as more beautiful. Women still wore tight corsets but the heavy draped bustle was abandoned.

Edwardian women were characterised by an S-bend figure and a large bosom. A corset had to be worn as the Edwardians valued a full 'hourglass' figure.

The Edwardian silhouette was soon questioned by Paul Poiret, the first designer to build a fashion empire. He replaced the strong boned corset with a softer version and created flowing forms that utilised the 'empire' line.

It is a myth of fashion history that women abandoned their corsets during the 1920s. Women wore cylindrical elastic corsets to fit the new silhouettes in fashion, to provide an unbroken line down the whole upper body.

The next major change was heavily influenced by Hollywood and the film industry. In the 1930s the bosom was back in fashion and women preferred softly sculptural clothes with accentuated feminine contours. This new shape was achieved by wearing shaped brassieres.

In the mid-1930s corseted crinolines and evening gowns with modified bustles were reintroduced. Royal dressmaker Norman Hartnell was a key figure in this neo-Victorian movement.

In 1947, at the end of the Second World War, Christian Dior launched his first and now legendary spring collection immortalised as the New Look. In fact the look was far from new as it revisited the tiny waist and whole circle skirts of the nineteenth century. At the time, everyone wanted to forget about the wartime styles that had been heavily influenced by the rationing of materials. The idea of extravagant amounts of fabric, long full skirts and cinching in women's waists seemed very new and appealing.

To achieve Dior's post-war New Look, corseted underwear to tighten the waist and specially created pads for the hips were used as a foundation to emphasise a strong feminine shape.

As much as the 1950s were elegant and feminine, the 60s were characterised by a cool style influenced by the music of the era. Fashion became youthful: bright colours, pop art, space age influences and synthetic fabrics were all 'in'.

By the liberated 1970s corseted bras and underskirts were used only for special occasions and eveningwear and this is still the case today. Corsets are no longer considered necessary and women prefer to shape their bodies by means of diet and exercise.

1900–9

1911

1912–13

1920

New Look

History of supported and structured garments > Supporting materials

Supporting materials

1   Canvas.

2   Fusible and non-fusible tape.

3   Iron-on interlining/fusing.

4   Rigid interlining for extreme
     support.

5   Tailor's front supporting piece
     with canvas and wadding.

The range of available supporting materials is vast. These days we still use the well-established technique of boning to support corsetry and underskirts. Creating thickness and bulk can also be achieved using wadding as an added layer to fabric.

You will find different weights of netting under a garment for bulk or lift. Padding can also be used to create shape and volume and to emphasise parts of the body. Padding can give more definition and form to a garment; quilted fabric will look crisp and stiff, standing away from the body and wadding can be used to create structure and insulation.

Interfacing/interlining is primarily used to support and add substance to fabric. It comes in two versions: fusible (iron-on) and non-fusible (sewn-in). On a traditional shirt, the collar, cuffs and button-fly would not be without its use. Canvas is also used as interfacing on parts of a garment that require more body, for example the front of a tailored jacket.

Fabrics such as organza, organdie and cotton muslin all work very well as backings for other fabrics that require body and stability.

Crinoline and rigid interlining stiffen and add solid support to sculpted garments.

It is interesting to research upholstery and curtain making to get some ideas of different materials and techniques. Books on equestrian wear, shoe or bag making also have lots of great ideas for inspiration when designing supported and structured garments.

6   Tailored shoulder pads.

7   Shoulder roll.

8   Crinoline.

9   Boning, plastic and metal with plastic coating.

10   Wadding.

11   Raglan shoulder pads.

Netting

Net is an open-mesh, transparent fabric. It is one of the oldest fabrics known, available in a variety of natural and man-made fibres, such as silk, cotton, rayon, polyester and nylon. It can range from very sheer to stiff and heavy. The finer version of netting is called tulle and shows a hexagonal pattern.

Netting is mainly used as a supporting material. It can be made into a petticoat or underskirt by gathering the netting into one or more layers of multi-tiered net. The amount used depends on the volume required. Netting can be used as an interfacing and underlining as it adds crispness without weight. It is also suitable as a base for lace appliqués. Net is not only used for the inside of garments – some variations give great effects when used for the final garment too.

Net has no grain line and has more give in the width than in the length. Remember this when cutting the fabric in order to get the best use out of it. Care must be taken when working with net as it has a tendency to rip easily. It does not fray, but a raw edge may irritate the wearer's skin. To prevent this, it can be finished with a binding, or a lace or net facing.

1

GIVENCHY

2

3

1   Givenchy haute couture, A/W03.

2   Design inspiration and illustration of a dress in netting for Givenchy haute couture, A/W03.

3   Dress made from different weight netting for Givenchy haute couture A/W03.

4   Different types of netting.

5   Christian Dior skirt with netting inlay attached for more volume.

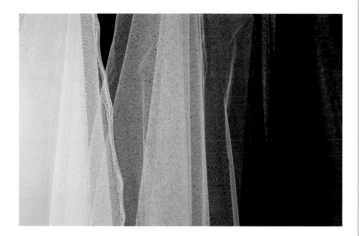

4

Netting varieties

Illusion is one of the finest nets and is often used as decoration on garments such as bridal veils.

Maline is a fine netting with hexagonal patterned holes. It is used mainly for millinery.

Point d'esprit is a fine net with dots on a repeated interval; it is mostly used for decoration.

Tulle is also a fine netting and can be used as is or it can be starched – such as for ballet tutus.

5

Quilting

Quilted fabrics are available in two-layered and three-layered versions. The two-layered version has a top or face layer made of decorative fabric. The second layer is wadding, which is made out of cotton or synthetic fibre batting. Traditionally, both layers are stitched together in a series of seam diagonals to form a diamond pattern. Two-layered quilting is mostly used for lining to insulate a garment.

A three-layered quilted fabric can be single-faced or double-faced. When single-faced the top or face layer is usually a decorative fabric over a lightweight tricot, lining or gauze backing. In between is a layer of wadding and all three layers are machine quilted together. The double-faced quilted fabric has two top or face layers and a layer of wadding sandwiched in between, all of which are machine quilted together.

Some quilting fabrics are thicker than others, depending on the separate layers and thickness of wadding. A quilted material appears stiff and crisp and stands away from the body. Some designers create their own quilted fabrics and stitching technique for a unique, decorative effect.

Quilt is also used as a means of protection, such as on motorcycling gear and other sports garments.

1   Marios Schwab, A/W07.

Padding

1   Evening dress by Elsa Schiaparelli (1890–1973).

2   A tailored shoulder pad (left) and a raglan shoulder pad (right).

3   Raglan and tailored shoulder pads in different shapes and sizes.

Padding a garment helps to emphasise parts of the body, to add shape and support or it can simply make a fashion statement. Padding involves creating a tunnel or shape, which then can be stuffed with lambswool, polyester fleece, cotton batting or armo wool. One early example of an exceptional use of padding is an evening dress by Elsa Schiaparelli (1890–1973), a designer with a strong interest in surrealism. The dress is a black skeleton evening gown, with a padded representation of human bones.

Christian Dior also created exceptional padded designs with his New Look collection. Here, he created pads to emphasise the hip for a stronger feminine look. Modern designers Victor & Rolf showed an experimental way of using padded sculptured pieces with garments draped on top in their 1998/1999 Autumn/Winter collection. The beauty of the concept was that all the clothes could be worn with or without the padded pieces.

Padding can also be used in hemlines, to soften and add weight and body to a hem. The advantage of a well-padded hem is that it provides protection from overpressing and keeps its softness for the lifetime of the garment.

1

Shoulder pads

A shoulder pad is used to define the shoulder area and create a smooth appearance over the shoulder and collarbone. Pads are used between the garment fabric and the lining, or covered pads can be used inside the garment on the shoulder.

Shoulder pads come in different sizes and shapes. Depending on the sleeve design, there are several shapes available. For example, the tailored pad is triangular and made from layers of wadding sandwiched between felt, which is then loosely stitched together. The tailored pads used in women's and men's jackets or coats are approximately 1–1.5cm high over the shoulder point. The height can be customised and layers can be added to accommodate a different look.

Pads are also available for raglan sleeves – a raglan sleeve has a much softer appearance and therefore the pad is an oval shape. The tailored pad used in a set-in sleeve is cut off at the end of the shoulder to create a strong and square appearance whereas the raglan shoulder pad runs along the shoulder and into the sleeve for a softer look.

Regular pads can be bought ready-made in haberdashery shops or, for a better result, can be created from scratch using the pattern of the garment so that the fit and form are perfect. Designers have to consider the extra costs when using a bespoke shoulder pad but such costs are likely to be counterbalanced by the creation of a better, perhaps more exciting silhouette.

During the 1980s and early 1990s shoulder pads were especially popular with fashion designers. Garments such as blouses and jersey pieces were available with detachable pads. Growing up in the 1980s, women would fill their accessory drawers with different sizes and shapes of shoulder pads that could then be added under all kinds of outfits.

Feminine tailoring
At the beginning of the 1980s a new clothing style was born. Famous women in US television programmes, such as *Dallas* and *Dynasty*, as well as influential women in politics and business made this style successful. It soon became popularly known as 'power dressing'. This is instantly recognisable by the use of expensive materials such as silk and a powerful, masculine cut. Both men and women wore suits and the style was intended to convey an impression of competence and authority.

3

2

Interlining/fusing

Interlining/fusing is used at certain parts of the garments to add body and stability. It is available as fusible interlining (adhesive dots that melt when ironed on to the fabric), or in a non-fusible form for sewing in. You will find more information about interlining and fusing on pages 166–167.

Where to use interlining and fusing

Some parts of a garment need reinforcement. Critical points, such as buttonholes and buttons for example, must be strengthened to enable them to withstand high levels of pulling. Areas such as the waistband on a skirt or trouser also need to be tough in order to stand up to all the movement experienced around this area. Collars and cuffs, which are expected to stand up and look the same after several launderings, will also need to be reinforced.

Reinforce the following areas by fusing:

Facings
Facing. Fuse completely the facing around the neckline and armhole.

The shirt
Shirt collar. Fuse under-collar, top-collar and collar stand.

Button stand. Fuse complete button stand.

Cuffs. Fuse complete cuff and cuff fly opening.

The trouser
Waistband. Fuse the complete waistband.

Belt loops. Fuse the complete belt loops.

Pocket. Fuse the pocket mouth with a 2–3cm stripe of fusing.

Zip fly. Fuse under wrap and over wrap of the zip fly.

The jacket
Front. Fuse the complete front with a fusible interfacing.

Collar. Fuse the collar and lapel with a stitch-reinforced fusing.

Front facing. Fuse completely with a stitch-reinforced fusing.

Pocket. Fuse the pocket mouth using a 2–3cm strip of stitch-reinforced fusing and interface the jets for the jetted pocket.

Back. Fuse the top of the back panels.

Sleeve. Fuse the top of the sleeve head and the button fly and hem facing.

Hem. Fuse the hem facing completely and 1cm past the breakline.

Vent. Fuse the complete under wrap of the vent and the facing of the over wrap.

The skirt
Waistband. Fuse the complete waistband.

Pocket. Fuse the pocket mouth and the jets for the jetted pocket.

Zip. Cut out a small circular shape of fusing and reinforce the zip end.

Vent. Fuse the complete under wrap of the vent and the facing of the over wrap.

Belts
Belt. Reinforce the complete belt.

Fusible interlining

There are three steps to note when using a fusible (iron-on) interlining.

Heat. The heat of the iron or fusing machine has to be compatible with the adhesive used on the interlining and the fabric.

Pressure. The fusing may not become attached to the fabric if the pressure is too low.

Time. Depending on the melting point of the adhesive and the pressure applied to the lining and fabric, the time has to be set right. If too little time is allowed the adhesive might not melt to the fabric.

Fusible interlinings are available in a variety of types to suit all kinds of fabrics. Some have adhesive dots close together for more body cover and less movement in the fabric, which adds stability. Some have adhesive dots further apart, which creates softer and more lightweight fusing in order to allow more flexibility in the fabric.

Thread reinforced interlining is also available in two versions. The first is horizontally and vertically reinforced interlining, which contains vertical threads for a high level of stability and horizontal threads for additional flexibility. The other kind of interlining contains only vertical threads, creating vertical stability. Both versions have a grain line following the thread so this must be considered when cutting out.

A range of specialised interlinings is also available. For example, leather and fur are sensitive to heat and should therefore be fused with an interlining that has an adhesive with a low melting point. Stretch fabrics, jersey and knitwear can be stabilised in every direction with a jersey fusing. Jersey fusing is also suitable for interlining loose-woven fabrics in order to retain the softness and movement of the fabric.

Non-fusible interlining

Non-fusible, sewn-in interlining achieves similar effects to the fusible variety. For a better result, some fabrics should be underlaid with materials such as muslin, organza, organdie or crinoline. For example, a full skirt on an evening gown made from silk duchess would benefit from an underlayer of silk organza, which adds support and permanent shape to the garment. Similarly, the use of an open-weave woollen or cotton fabric between the lining and outer fabric in a winter coat would create extra warmth.

Classic shirts make extensive use of interlining to support the collar, cuffs and button stand. On a trouser or skirt the waistband, facing, pocket mouth, zip-fly and sometimes the hem are often interlined. The collar, lapel, facing, pocket mouth, fastening, vent and hemline of a jacket or coat would also be supported in this way.

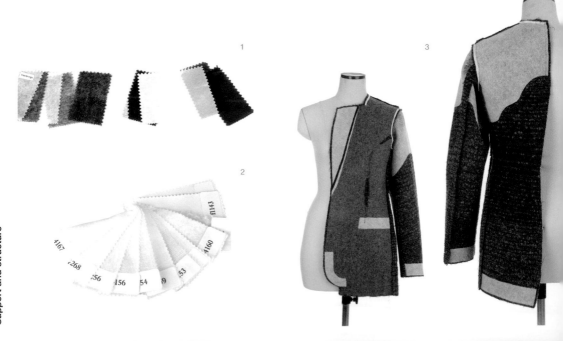

1

2

3

Canvas interfacing

Canvas is another type of interfacing, which can be set between the lining, facing and outer fabric. It is used where the garment requires more body and long-lasting shape. Canvas is a combination of hair and wool threads with horsehair twists or viscose filaments. For supporting the pockets, the use of a linen canvas or linen/hair canvas is advisable. It will support the pocket mouth so that it stays permanently in shape.

Canvas is also used as interfacing in traditional jackets and coats to support the shape of the jacket (rather than the shape of the person wearing it). The purpose of the canvas is to control the fabric and reduce its tendency to wrinkle and stretch.

Canvas was, and still is, used in corsets and underskirts.

1   Different samples of fusible interlining.

2   Different samples of non-fusible interlining.

3   Examples of a jacket that has been fused to add support and body to the fabric and shape of the jacket.

4   Jacket inside, canvas as chest piece and shoulder support.

5   Canvas samples.

6   Pre-finished canvas piece.

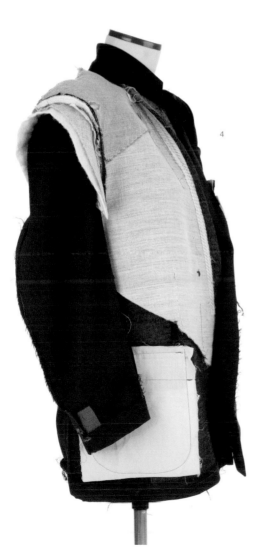

4

5

6

Corsetry

1/2 1940s/50s bras with waist support.

3 1930s girdle with support for waist to hip by elastic fabric.

A corset is a close-fitting bodice, stiffened with boning. The role of the corset is to shape the body and to impose a fashionable silhouette upon it. The word was used during the seventeenth and eighteenth centuries but became more common in the nineteenth century, replacing the word 'corps'. Over time, corsetry would be used to control and shape three main areas of a body: the bust, waist and hips. Corsetry often worked against nature and therefore created an illusion.

Boning

Boning was originally made from whalebone in constructed undergarments such as corsetry. Today we have a choice of two materials: metal or plastic. Rigilene O is a particular type of plastic boning made from fine polyester rods.

Metal boning needs a casing or tunnel prepared; the bone slides into it and is therefore covered up. Plastic boning can be stitched onto the foundation and only needs covering up on the cutting-off lines.

Depending on the style of corset, boning can be placed from the hip to the waist, and into and around the bust. The boning can be stitched on to the wrong side of the outer fabric as a design effect or worked into the foundation of the corset.

4　A selection of traditional and modern boning materials:

　　Rigilene (a)
　　Metal (b)
　　Plastic (c)

5/6　Samples of a corset with rigilene boning to provide bust, waist and abdomen support.

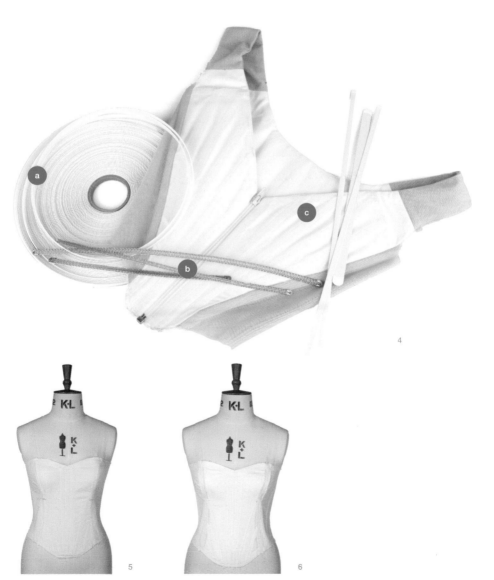

4

5

6

Materials for constructing a corset

Cotton drill is a strong natural material with flexibility. The twill weave is one of the stronger weave techniques and fabric made in this way is therefore suitable for a foundation of a corset. It provides the base for applying the boning.

Mesh is a stretch powernet made of synthetic fibre, used to give more flexibility.

Canvas is a substantial material made from a combination of hair and wool threads with horsehair twists or viscose filaments. It is used in corsetry to control the fabric and reduce its tendency to wrinkle and stretch.

Interlining/fusing is a woven or non-woven fabric that can be ironed on or sewn in to support and add substance to any fabric used for the foundation of a corset.

Brushed cotton is a light cotton fabric that is brushed on one side of the fabric to achieve a soft and cushioned effect. It is placed between the boned foundation of the corset and the outer fabric to prevent the boning from showing through.

Supporting materials are used when the natural body of the outer fabric is not strong enough. Fabrics such as muslin, organza and organdie are used for support. The supporting

materials would be mounted (mounting stitches are medium hand stitches around the edge of the fabric piece) and the two fabrics used as one.

Lining is a very thin fabric made of silk, viscose or synthetic fibres. Its purpose is to protect the skin from the boned foundation and to clean up the inside of the corset for a good quality finish.

Laces, hook-and-eye fastenings and zips can all be used to fasten corsetry.

1

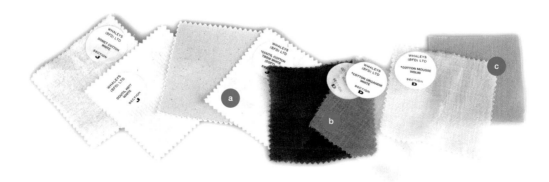

1 A selection of materials for constructing a corset:

Cotton drill (a)
Organza (b)
Mesh powernet (c)

2

3

4

2   One-piece strapless corset with lace fastening in the back and hook-and-eye in the centre front.

3   Corselet foundation with boning, powernet and inner belt, fasten by hook-and-eye underneath the zip and garters.

4   The inside of a black velvet corset by Vivienne Westwood, with boning in the centre front and centre back, powernet as side panels and straps and a zip fastening.

Creating volume

Adding volume to a garment means changing the dimensions to create a larger silhouette. This can be done by adding volume through seams and darts or gathers, pleats and drapes, as well as by adding flare. The right fabrics can also help to increase the volume on a garment.

Volume through drapes

Draping techniques can be used to achieve a soft look with added volume. A drape is excess fabric falling down (draping) from one anchor point or between two or more anchor points. The cowl drape is one of the more controlled drapes and works well on tops, sleeves or skirts. Irregular and uncontrolled drapes can also be created. These are done on the mannequin and not as a flat pattern construction.

Volume through flare

A flared garment is fitted at one point, such as the waist, and gradually widens to the other end of the garment, such as the hemline of a skirt. Flare in a garment is usually loose swinging and not controlled through pleats or gathers. The method used to add flare to a garment can be slash and spread or by simply adding on flare to the seams, such as the side seam, and ignoring darts such as the waist dart.

Volume through fabric

Using the right fabric for a garment that has been designed to come off the body shape is important. If the garment achieves more volume through drapes, gathers or pleats, more fabric needs to be provided. On the other hand, if volume is added by cut and construction, such as for a sculptured piece, the right weight, texture and density of the fabric is essential.

1

1   Haute couture dress by
     Christian Lacroix, S/S08.
     Catwalking.com.

2   Dress by Julien Macdonald.

2

Creating volume with godets

Seams and darts are not only used
for shaping a garment to the body,
but also for expanding shape away
from the body. Seams can be used
to add in extra pieces of fabric for
more volume, such as godets.

A godet is traditionally a triangular-
shaped piece of fabric set into a
seam or a cut line. Godets are used
to add extra fullness as much as
being a design feature. The shape of
a godet varies – it can be pointed,
round or even squared on the top
and constructed as a half-, three-
quarter- or full-circle.

The most common use of godets is
in skirts, but they can also be added
into sleeves, trouser bottoms,
bodices and so on.

When stitching in a pointed godet,
extra care needs to be taken with the
top point. Seam allowance can be
limited and the top point can tear
easily and fray. It is therefore
advisable to strengthen the top point
with interlining before sewing in the
godet. To achieve a pointed top, first
stitch one side of the godet from the
hemline to the top point and secure,
then take it out of the sewing
machine and start again on the other
side, from hemline to the top point.
Try this first on a sample piece of
fabric before attempting to sew the
final garment.

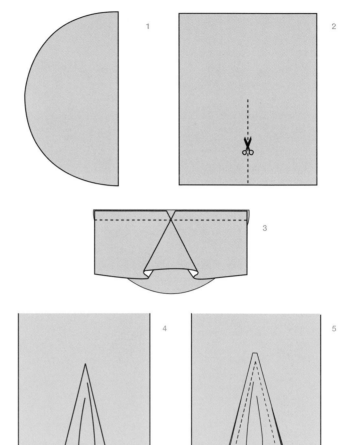

1   Circle-shaped godet.

2   Cutting line on garment.

3   Straighten out the cutting
     line to insert the godet.

4   Good side of the garment.

5   Wrong side of the garment.

6   Dress with godets by
     Julien Macdonald.

6

Creating volume with gore panels

The gore skirt has a similar look to the godet skirt except that there are no inserts. The skirt is wide at the hem and shaped to the waist. A gore skirt can start with four gores, which have seams at the sides, centre front and centre back and there can be as many as 24 gores in a skirt. Depending on the look, the gores are equally spaced or random. The skirt may hang straight from the hip or any point below, be flared or pleated or have an uneven hemline.

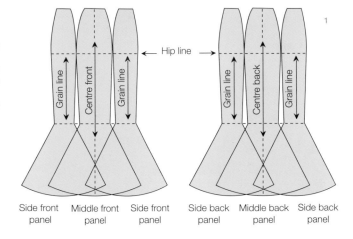

Side front panel   Middle front panel   Side front panel   Side back panel   Middle back panel   Side back panel

1   Pattern pieces for a six-piece gore skirt.

2   Skirt with gore panels by Julien Macdonald, A/W05.

3   Childrenswear dress by AFI, Anette Fischer with gathers on sleeve head and side part of lower waist.

4   Section of pleated skirt by Boudicca haute couture, S/S08. Catwalking.com.

Creating volume through gathers and pleats

Applying gathers is a great way of creating volume.

- Take the fabric edge that is meant to be gathered and place under the sewing machine. Turn the stitch length to the largest stitch (4–5mm).

- Start sewing about 5–7mm away from the fabric edge. Sew from the start to the finish of the gathering line. Sew a second line a couple of millimetres below the first.

- Take the top threads from both sewing lines and pull.

- As you pull the thread the fabric will bunch up and create gathers, which can be equally spaced or irregular depending on the design.

Pleats, like gathers, will create instant volume. A pleat is folded fabric, held down securely along joining seam lines. It can be pressed down or left soft. The volume created by pleats depends on the number of pleats and the pleat depth.

4

3

1

1   Calico sample with
    experimental pleating by
    Laurel Robinson.

2   Research book and design
    images by Laurel Robinson.

2

1

2

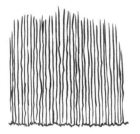

3

1 Dress by Puccini with
   sunray pleated detail
   under the arm.

2 Crystal pleats.

3 Tree bark pleats.

4 Sunray pleats.

5 Box pleats.

6 Plain knife pleats.

7 Accordian pleats.

4

6

5

7

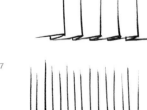

1 Buttons can be used to great decorative effect.

'I'm a very restless person. I'm always doing something.
The creative process never stops.'

Oscar de la Renta

This chapter will look at the 'finishing touch'. A garment can be
faced, bound or left with a raw edge. The look and feel of the
finishes can make or break a garment. Good knowledge of
fastenings, linings, fabric behaviour, traditional techniques and
specific fabric finishings is always necessary. Some designers
have created their own finishing techniques to give a unique
look to their creations. For example, Levi's uses its back pocket
stitching as a trademark.

Linings

1   Back view of a women's jacket by Ted Baker (S/S08), shown inside out to expose the centre back pleat in the lining for comfort.

2   Women's jacket by Ted Baker (S/S08), shown inside out, to expose a lovely finish. Lining and front facing are sewn together with a pink binding in between. The inside chest pocket uses jets and a pink lining triangle to cover up the button (which fastens the inside pocket). This prevents the button from rubbing on the garment and damaging it.

3   Men's jacket by Ted Baker (S/S08), shown inside out. A men's jacket offers more inside pockets than the women's. This particular jacket has a pocket for small change with a concealed zip on the bottom right side between the lining and facing. It also has a chest pocket for a wallet, a pocket for a mobile phone and additional spare pockets.

4   Women's trousers by Ted Baker (S/S08), shown inside out to display the half lining from waist to knee.

A lining can be added to a garment as an extra layer for several different purposes – to ensure that the shape of the garment is retained, for warmth or for design and comfort. It will also hide all the internal construction details. A lining can be worked in and can either cover the whole of the garment or act as a half lining. It can also be detachable as a zip-in or button-in version. Usually, jackets, coats, skirts and trousers are lined. The lining fabric can vary from silk and cotton to fur.

It is just as important to design the inside of a garment as the outside. Attention to detail is vital!

1

2

3

4

5

6

7

8

5   Casual jacket by Joseph (S/S08).

6   Joseph jacket shown inside out. It is half lined in the front, from shoulder to chest level. The sleeves are lined for comfort and this also makes it easier to slip into the jacket. The seams in the front and the pocket are bound for a neat finish.

7   The back of the Joseph jacket is completely lined.

8   This skirt lining hem has been finished with a lace trimming, showing attention to detail.

How to pattern cut a jacket lining

In most cases, linings have the same shape as the garment.

- When cutting the pattern for a jacket, the facings of the front are taken off the lining pattern.

- Some tailors add a small pleat at mid-armhole level on the lining frontpiece, to accommodate the force that the lining pocket creates.

- At the hemline of the lining pattern, 1cm is added to the finished hemline of the garment in order to create a pleat for extra comfort.

- The ease provided in the sleeve head is taken into a pleat or dart in the lining sleeve as the lining fabric cannot be eased into the armhole as easily as the outer garment fabric.

- The lining needs to cover the bulk of the seam allowance inside a garment, so 1cm is added to the side seams of the body and sleeve.

- A pleat is added for comfort in the centre back of the lining pattern.

- Sometimes a tough quality of lining is used for the sleeve (twill weave, for example), as there is a lot of movement and friction around the elbow area.

Facings

1   Dress by Joseph, S/S08, shown inside out to display a faced neckline and armhole.

2   The gathered centre part in the front neckline of the Joseph dress is turned into small darts at the facing.

A facing is used to finish a raw edge on a garment. It is mostly used when the edge is shaped, such as on a neckline. The facing is cut to the same shape as the edge line, stitched on and folded to the inner side. Facings are commonly added to areas such as the neckline, the armhole on a sleeveless garment, openings at the front and back or a hemline. Usually the facing is cut in the same fabric as the garment and then lightly fused, but it can also be cut in a contrasting fabric or colour to the garment.

1

2

Fastenings

1   Dress detail by Dolce & Gabbana (S/S08), fastened in the centre front with a hook-and-eye tape.

2   Hook-and-eye fastening on the neckline of a dress. It is placed at the end of the zip to hold the neckline in place.

3   Jacket and dress by Dolce & Gabbana (S/S08). The jacket is fastened with large poppers.

4   Silk dress by Ted Baker (S/S08), fastened with a rouleau loop and button, as well as a concealed zip in the left side seam.

5   Silk top by Hugo Boss (S/S08), fastened in the centre front by rouleau loops and covered buttons.

6   A dress with a concealed zip in the centre back.

7   A printed top by Ted Baker (S/S08), fastened on the neckline with a stitched tunnel and a decorative satin tie.

8   Jacket by Hugo Boss (S/S08), fastened in the centre front with bound buttonholes and covered buttons.

9   Detail shot of a bound buttonhole.

Fastenings are functional items that will keep a garment closed. They can be hidden or made into a focal point. The family of fastenings is diverse, ranging from buttons, press studs, Velcro and magnets to buckles, hook-and-eye fastenings and zips. The choice of fastenings will dramatically influence the style of a garment. Avoid settling for your first idea and have a good look at what the market has to offer.

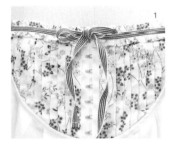
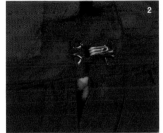

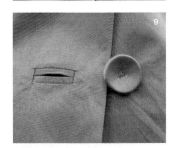

The shirt

Traditionally, a shirt is closed by small buttons and buttonholes, although the buttons can come in different sizes. The buttonhole stand can be worked with visible or concealed buttonholes. Cuffs are also closed with a button and buttonhole.

1

2

Trousers

For a casual look, use an elasticated waistband or a tunnel and cord. For a tailored solution use a waistband with an underwrap, closing with a hook fastening or a button and buttonhole. The zip can be placed either in the centre front or the side seam up to the waistband and is covered from one side. Trouser waistbands are usually finished with belt loops to accommodate a belt.

The skirt

Skirts can be fastened in various ways. When finished with a waistband, an underwrap can be created with a hook fastening or button and buttonhole. The zip opening (which reaches up to the waistband) would be sewn in, either concealed or with one or both sides covered.

If the zip is taken to the top of the waistline, use a small loop and button or a hook-and-eye fastening on the very top of the zip to ensure that it stays closed.

A skirt waistline can also be held in place by an elasticised waistband or a tunnel-and-cord finish. If you are seeking a different look, use a wrap closing, where the skirt is closed by one side wrapping over the other.

3

4

1   Detail showing a button stand with concealed buttonholes.

2   Different fastening options for trousers.

3   Skirt shown inside out to display full lining.

4   The skirt has a tunnel-and-cord fastening.

Haberdashery

Fastenings and trimmings such as buttons, zips, elastics, studs and rivets are only some of the endless list of haberdashery. Haberdashery can be functional and/or decorative and will change with fashion. It can also make or spoil an outfit and control the fit of the garment.

Zips

It is important to choose the right zip for the garment being constructed. You can get zips with metal teeth), which are on a cotton or synthetic tape. These zips are strong and can be used for medium- to heavyweight fabrics. A lighter option is a synthetic polyester or nylon zip with plastic teeth, attached to a woven tape. An open-ended zip with either metal or plastic teeth can be used for jackets and coats. Concealed zips have plastic teeth and are easy to attach to garments.

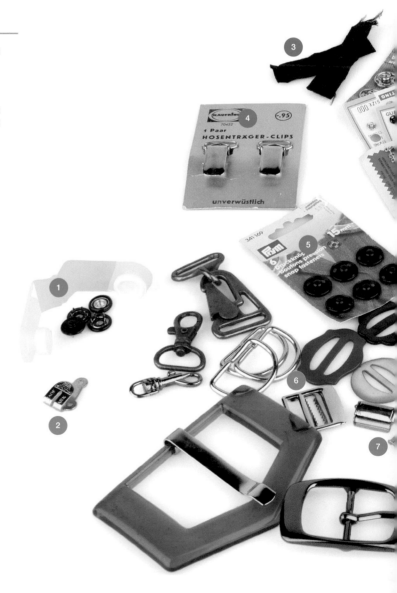

1   Non-sew poppers or snap fasteners.

2   Skirt hook. This must be sewn on by hand.

3   Popper or snap-fastener tape. This can be sewn on by machine.

4   Clips for braces.

5   Popper or snap fastener. This must be sewn on by hand.

6   Buckles and clips.

7   Brace clips.

8   Hook-and-eye fastenings. These must be sewn on by hand.

Buttons and closures

Buttons are available in all kinds of materials such as glass, plastic, metal, leather, mother-of-pearl or covered with fabric. When sewing on a flat button with two to four holes, make sure to include the thread shank. It will be needed on most fabrics to give space for the underwrap (buttonhole layer) to lie flat beneath the fastened button. Closures, such as poppers and hooks, can be used as well as buttons. Here is just a selection of the variety of closures.

9   Pre-finished frog fastenings, one with a Chinese button and the other with a hook and loop attached.

10   Decorative zip puller to hook on to the zip head.

11   Hook-and-eye tape. This can be sewn on by machine.

12   Basic buckle that can be covered with fabric.

13   Sew-on leather coat hangers

14   Non-sew hook and bar for skirt and trousers.

15   A selection of zips.

Decorations and trimmings

1   Different kinds of decoration and trimmings, ready for application.

2   A selection of bugle beads, sequins, pearls and beads in different sizes.

3   A box of pearl beads, nylon thread and wire for attaching the beads. When embroidering, use a slim hand sewing needle to make sure the needle fits through the hole of the bead.

Decorations such as beads, sequins, rosettes, bows and trimmings come in and out of fashion. Finding the right balance is not easy and sometimes less is more.

Ready-made decorations can be hand sewn or machine stitched on to the garment. Most of them are great fun for children's wear.

Trimmings for all kind of finishes are available in haberdashery shops. Some trimmings are elastic and can be used in lingerie and swimwear or as waistbands and cuffs on casual wear. Others are non-stretch like petersham ribbon, woven jacquard ribbon, silken braids and piping.

Lace trimmings can be exposed or used in the underlayers of an outfit, for example on lingerie. The lace trimming can be manufactured in different ways.

Embroidery can be used to decorate a garment. It is time consuming but worthwhile. Many designers have the work done abroad, in order to keep the costs down. There is a vast choice of beads, sequins, pearls and bugle beads on the market, but do not forget that your creative eye might identify other materials that can be embroidered on to a garment.

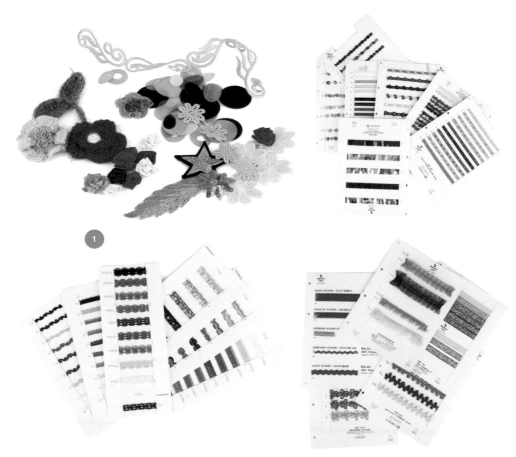

1

4   Elasticated lace for lingerie.

5   Beaded lace edging is finished on both edges with a fine lace border and pearl bead decoration.

6   Netted lace whereby the base is netting.

7   Crocheted lace or broderie anglaise, which is an open-work, embroidered cotton trim that can be finished on one or both sides.

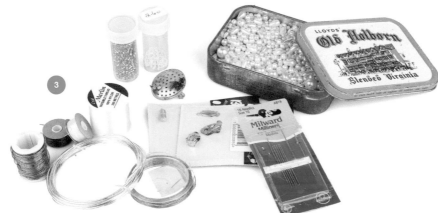

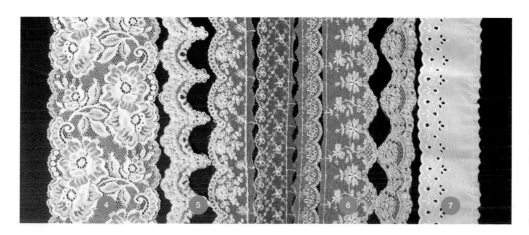

1

This book has taken a journey through all the most important areas of garment construction, starting with the challenging skill of pattern cutting and moving on to the specialist areas of couture, tailoring and industrial methods, through to draping on the mannequin and a detailed examination of the various tools and techniques that can be employed. I hope that this will awaken your interest and encourage you to try out some exciting shapes on the pattern table and mannequin stand.

If you intend to develop your garment construction skills, it is a good idea to start a sample box for collecting all kinds of samples, such as interlinings, shoulder pads, tapes and so on. Make sure that you label your samples so that you know which shop you found them in. This will be very helpful and should, in the long run, save you time running around.

It is hoped that this book will encourage you to become more curious about garment construction and inspire you to start your own investigations. However, please remember one thing: learn the basics first and then start experimenting. Always question what you are doing and why you are doing it.

Batting
Tangled fibre sheets used in quilting and stuffing.

Bespoke
Custom-made, one-off tailored garments.

Block (also known as a sloper)
A 2D template, constructed using measurements taken from a size chart or an individual model. It has no style lines or seam allowance.

Boning
Method for stiffening foundation garments, like bodices for dresses. The metal or plastic strips called bones were originally made from whalebone.

Brassiere
An undergarment worn by women to mould and support the breasts. Now known as the bra.

Breakline
The folding line of a collar.

Breeches
Trousers worn by men until the late nineteenth century.

Bustle
Nineteenth-century undergarment that supported back fullness in skirts, using pads, cushions or arrangement of steel springs attached below the waist at the back of a woman's dress.

Canvas
A combination of hair and wool threads with horsehair twists or viscose filaments. Canvas is used for creating body and long-lasting shape in a garment.

Calico
A cheap cotton fabric, available in different weights, used for making toiles.

Classic
A garment that has a widespread acceptance over a period of time and is well known by name (such as the little black dress, for example).

Course
The horizontal (crosswise) ridge of a knitted fabric.

Crinoline
Stiff underskirt from the 1840s and 1850s. Stiffness was achieved using crinoline fabric, often combined with horsehair for extra rigidity.

Darts
Darts control excess fabric to create shape on a garment when stitched together to a zero or pivotal point.

Ease
An allowance added to a pattern in order to allow for extra comfort or movement.

Elastomers
A synthetic material that has extensibility with complete elastic recovery.

Facing
Used to finish a raw edge of a garment. Facings are mostly used when the edge is shaped, for example on a neckline.

Felting
The knotting together of fibres (using heat or friction and chemicals) to produce a matted material.

Finishes
Processes and techniques that
are used to manipulate the
appearance, characteristics,
performance or handle of a fabric.
Also the way a garment is neatened
during construction, for example
with seams and hems.

Gathering
Two parallel loosely stitched rows
that are pulled up to create fullness
and a decorative, ruffled effect.

Grain line
A grain line indicates the direction in
which a pattern piece is laid onto
fabric before being cut out.

Girdle
Ladies' undergarment created in the
1930s in order to shape and hold
the lower part of the female body,
occasionally including the legs.

Gauze
Loose-woven fabric made of loosely
twisted cotton yarns. Garments are
often given a crinkled finish and are
worn unpressed.

Grading
The increase or decrease of a
pattern size.

Godet
Panel of fabric inserted into a
garment, such as a skirt or dress,
to create flare.

Gore
Fabric panels used in garment
construction to add structure
and flare.

Haute couture
Garments made to measure for a
specific customer.

Holes and notches
These indicate where the separate
pieces of fabric will be attached to
one another.

House model
A male or female model with the
body shape that a designer works
towards.

Hoops
A hoop-shaped structure made up
of a series of round or oval circles
(whalebone, wire, or cane) gradually
increasing in size from top to
bottom.

Horsehair
Long, very coarse hair from the
mane and tail of a horse, used in
structural fabrics and wadding.

'Hourglass' figure
A body shape or garment with a full
bust, pinched-in waist and full,
curving hips, representing the
shape of an hourglass.

Interlining/fusing
This is a woven or non-woven fabric
that is used between the lining and
the outer fabric of a garment. It is
either fusible (iron-on) or non-fusible
(to be sewn-in).

Knife pleats
Pressed pleats that go in one
direction.

Lapel
The decorative rever of a tailored
jacket.

Glossary

Lining
Fabric used on the inside of a garment to hide the construction. It extends the garment's life as it helps to retain the shape. It also makes the garment more comfortable to wear.

Nap
Fibre ends that stick out on the surface of the fabric, making it soft to the touch. These fabrics, such as velvet, corduroy, fur and brushed cotton, must be cut in one direction only.

Netting
Net is an open-mesh, transparent fabric. It can range from very sheer to stiff and heavy.

Overlocking
Quick and efficient way of stitching, trimming and edging fabrics in a single action to neaten seams.

Pad stitching
A pad stitch is used to join two layers of materials together, using a diagonal stitch that is staggered from one row to the next.

Padding
Extra bulk in a garment used to emphasise parts of the body as well as adding shape and support.

Pattern
Initially developed from a design sketch using a block. A designer or pattern cutter adapts the block to create a pattern that includes style lines, drapes, pleats, pockets and other adjustments.

Petticoat
Ladies' undergarment, firstly worn under the skirt (between the sixteenth and seventeenth centuries) and later worn visibly as an outer-garment (between the seventeenth and eighteenth centuries).

Pret-à-porter
French term used in fashion design to describe ready-to-wear.

Quilting
Traditionally, quilting is made up of layers that are stitched together in a series of seam diagonals to form a diamond pattern. Quilting fabrics are available in two-layered and three-layered variations. The two-layered version has a top or face layer made of decorative fabric. The second layer is wadding, made out of cotton or synthetic fibre batting.

Sample
The first version of a garment made in the main fabric.

Scye
Technical name for the sleeve head.

Seam allowance
Seam allowance is added to seams to allow for stitching. These allowances vary depending on the kind of seam used and are usually facing the inside of a garment.

Slash and spread
A method used to add extra volume and flare.

Stand
A dressmaking mannequin or dummy.

Superlock
A very fine and tight overlocking stitch used on knit and jersey fabrics. It creates a wavy edge.

Tanning
A process for treating leather by removing the hair of the skin and revealing the grain.

Tier
Originating from the word attire, a tier is headwear made of gold and gems worn on pomp occasions since the fifteenth century.

Toile
The fabric sample used for fitting a garment. A toile has no finished seams, no fastenings such as buttonholes and buttons and no lining or facings.

Top-stitch
To stitch on the right side of the garment.

Tricot
Wrap-knit fabric made with two different yarns. It has fine wales on the front and crosswise ribs on the back.

Trunk hose
A short puffy trouser worn by men, with a pair of dense tights in the mid-sixteenth century.

Underpressing
The action whereby the iron is slipped between the hemming and outer fabric.

Wales
The vertical ridges in a knitted fabric.

Welt
The reinforced or decorative border of a garment or pocket.

Bibliography

Aldrich W. (2004)
Metric Pattern Cutting
WileyBlackwell

Amaden-Crawford C (2005)
The Art of Fashion Draping
Fairchild Publications, Inc.

Arnold J (1977)
**Patterns of Fashion:
Englishwomen's Dresses &
Their Construction**
Drama Publishers

Barbier M and Hanif-Boucher S
(2005)
The Story of Lingerie
Parkstone Press Ltd

Baudot F (1997)
Paul Poiret
Thames and Hudson

Burda (1988)
**Burda perfekt selbstschneidern
(Broschiert)**
Burda Medien Vertrieb

Cabrera R and Flaherty Meyers P
(1983)
**Classic Tailoring Techniques:
A Construction Guide for
Men's Wear**
Fairchild Books

Cabrera R and Flaherty Meyers P
(1984)
**Classic Tailoring Techniques:
A Construction Guide for
Women's Wear**
Fairchild Books

Capucci R (1996)
Roberto Capucci al teatro farnese
Progretti museali

Cicolini A (2007)
The New English Dandy
Thames and Hudson

Cloake D (2000)
**Lingerie Design on the Stand:
Designs for Underwear &
Nightwear**
Batsford

Coates C (1997)
Designer Fact File
British Fashion Council

Creative Publ. Intl. (2005)
**Tailoring: A Step-by-step Guide
to Creating Beautiful Customised
Garments**
Apple Press

de Rethy E and Perreau J (1999)
Monsieur Dior et nous: 1947–1957
Anthese

Doyle R (1997)
**Waisted Efforts: An Illustrated
Guide to Corset Making**
Sartorial Press Publications

Hawkins D (1986)
**Creative Cutting, Easy Ways to
Design and Make Stylish Clothes**
Everyman Ltd

Hunnisett J (1991)
**Period Costume for Stage and
Screen: Patterns for Women's
Dress: 1500–1800**
Players Press

Jefferys C (2003)
The Complete Book of Sewing
DK Publishing

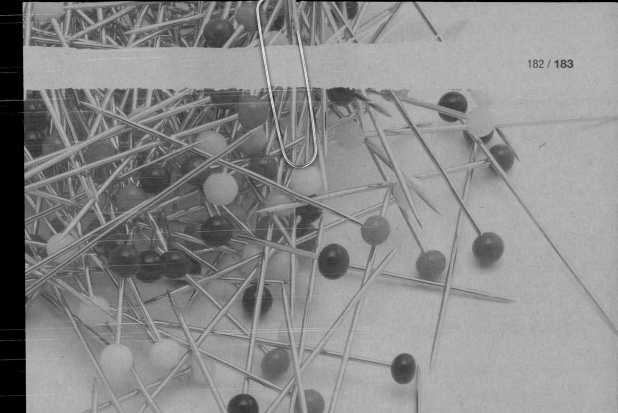

Jenkyn Jones S (2005)
Fashion Design
Laurence King Publishing

Joseph-Armstrong H (2005)
**Pattern Making for Fashion
Design**
Pearson Education

Jouve M-A (1997)
Balenciaga
Thames and Hudson

Kennett F (1985)
Secrets of the Couturiers
Orbis

Kirke B (1997)
Madeleine Vionnet
Chronicle Books

Langle E (2005)
**Pierre Cardin: Fifty Years of
Fashion and Design**
Thames and Hudson

Major J and Teng Y (2003)
**Yeohlee: Work, Material,
Architecture**
Peleus Press

Mankey C and Tortora P (2003)
Fairchild's Dictionary of Fashion
Fairchild Books

Martin R (1997)
Charles James
Thames and Hudson

Mondoo V (2004)
Black in Fashion
V&A Publications

Shaeffer C (2001)
Couture Sewing Techniques
Taunton Press Inc.

Shaeffer C (2008)
Fabric Sewing Guide
Krause Publications

Taylor P and Shoben M (2004)
**Grading for the Fashion Industry:
The Theory and Practice**
Shoben Fashion Media

Tomoko N (2005)
Pattern Magic Vol. 1

Tomoko N (2007)
Pattern Magic Vol. 2

Sorger R and Udale J (2006)
**The Fundamentals of Fashion
Design**
AVA Publishing

Wolff C (1996)
The Art of Manipulating Fabric
KP Books

Useful resources

Bata Shoe Museum
327 Bloor Street West
Toronto
Ontario
Canada M5S 1W7

www.batashoemuseum.ca

Costume Gallery
Los Angeles County Museum of Art
5905 Wilshire Boulevard
Los Angeles
CA 90036
USA

www.lacma.org

Costume Institute
Metropolitan Museum of Art
1000 5th Avenue at 82nd Street
New York
NY 10028-0198
USA

www.metmuseum.org

Galeria del costume
Amici di palazzo pitti
Piazza Pitti 1
50125 Firenze
Italy

www.polomuseale.firenze.it

Kobe Fashion Museum
Rokko Island
Kobe
Japan

www.fashionmuseum.or.jp

Kyoto Costume Institute
103, Shichi-jo
Goshonouchi Minamimachi
Kyoto 600-8864
Japan

www.kci.or.jp

MoMu
Antwerp Fashion Modemuseum
Nationalestraat 28
2000 Antwerpen
Belgium

www.momu.be

Musée de la mode et du costume
10 avenue Pierre 1 er de serbie
75116 Paris
France

Musée des Arts decoratifs
Musee des Arts de la mode et du
textile
107 rue de rivoli
75001 Paris
France

www.ucad.fr

**Musée des tissus et des arts
decoratifs de Lyon**
34 rue de la charite
F-69002 Lyon
France

www.musee-des-tissus.com

**Museum at the Fashion Institute
of Technology**
7th Avenue at 27th Street
New York
NY 10001-5992
USA

www.fitnyc.edu/museum

Construction

**Museum fuer Kunst und
Gewerbe Hamburg**
Steintorplatz
20099 Hamburg
Germany

www.mkg-hamburg.de

Museum of Costume
Assembly Rooms
Bennett Street
Bath, BA1 2QH
UK

www.museumofcostume.co.uk

**Museum of Fine Arts, Boston
Avenue of the Arts**
465 Huntington Avenue
Boston
Massachusetts 02115-5523
USA

www.mfa.org

Museum Salvatore Ferragamo
Palazzo Spini Feroni
Via Tornabuoni 2
Florence 50123
Italy

www.salvatoreferragamo.it

Victoria and Albert Museum (V&A)
Cromwell Road
South Kensington
London SW7 2RL
UK

www.vam.ac.uk

Wien Museum
Fashion collection with public library
(view by appointment)
A-1120 Vienna
Hetzendorfer
Strasse 79
Austria

www.wienmuseum.at

Useful resources

PUBLICATIONS AND MAGAZINES

10

Another Magazine

Arena Homme

Bloom

Collezioni

Dazed and Confused

Drapers Record

Elle

Elle Decoration

ID

In Style

International Textiles

Marie Claire

Marmalade

Numero Magazine

Oyster

Pop

Selvedge

Tank

Textile View

View on Colour

Viewpoint

Visionaire

Vogue

W

WWD Women's Wear Daily

WEBSITES

www.costumes.org

www.fashionoffice.org

www.promostyl.com

www.fashion.about.com

www.style.com

www.fashion-era.com

www.wgsn-edu.com

www.londonfashionweek.co.uk

www.premierevision.fr

www.hintmag.com

www.infomat.com

www.catwalking.com

www.showstudio.com

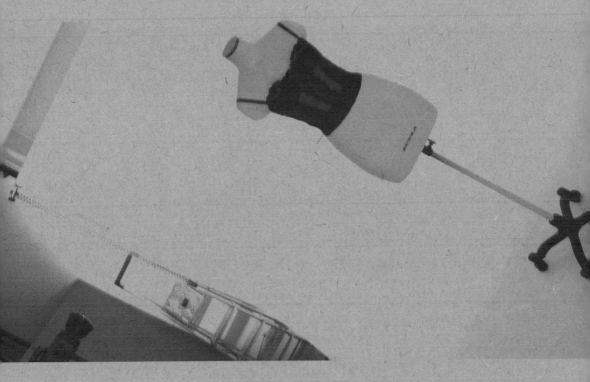

FASHION FORECASTING

www.londonapparel.com

www.itbd.co.uk

www.modeinfo.com

www.wgsn-edu.com

www.peclersparis.com

www.edelkoort.com

FASHION TRADE SHOWS

www.premierevision.fr

www.indigosalon.com

www.pittimmagine.com

www.purewomenswear.co.uk

www.magiconline.com

FASHION EMPLOYMENT AGENCIES

www.denza.co.uk

www.smithandpye.com

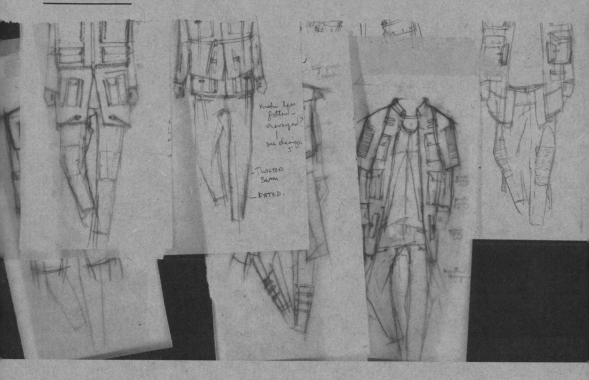

SHOPS AND SUPPLIERS

Barnet & Lawson
(Beaded trims, lace, ribbon)
16-17 Little Portland Street,
London W1
Tel: 020 7636 8591

Bead Shop
(Beads)
Covent Garden, London
Tel: 020 7240 0931

D.M Buttons
(Buttons)
D'arbley Mews, London
Tel: 020 7437 8897

**Freudenberg Nonwoven LP
Vilene Interlinings**
(Iron-on and sewn-in
interlining/fusing)
Lowfields Business Park, Elland,
West Yorkshire HX5 5DX
Tel: 01422 327900
Fax: 01422 327999

G&I Buttons
(Buttons)
Wardour Mews, London

John Lewis
(Fabrics, crafts, haberdashery)
Oxford Street, London
Tel: 020 7629 7711

Johnson Sewing Machines
(Sewing machine sales and services)
106 Woodvile Road,
New Barnet Herts EN5 5NJ
Tel: 020 8441 7603

Kleins
(Haberdashery, adjustable zips)
5 Noel Street W1
Tel: 020 7437 6162
(Haberdashery, trimmings)
Tel: 020 7790 2233

Liberty
(Fabrics, crafts, haberdashery)
Regent Street, London
Tel: 020 7734 1234

London Graphic Centre
(Artists' materials)
16-18 Shelton Street,
London WC2H 9JJ
Tel: 020 7240 0095/6

MacCulloch & Wallis
(Fabrics, crafts, haberdashery)
25-26 Dering Street,
London W1,
Tel: 020 7629 0311

Material World
(Fabric shop)
Camden High Street, London

Morplan
(Pattern cutting equipment)
56 Great Titchfield Street
London, W1W 7DF
Tel: 020 7636 1887

Perivale Guttermann Ltd
(Threads)
Wandsworth Road Greenford,
Middlesex UB6 7JS
Tel: 020 8998 5000

PFAFF Bellow
(Sewing machines and accessories)
Bellow House Ellerby Lane,
Leeds L59 8LE
Tel: 0113 244 2011

Construction

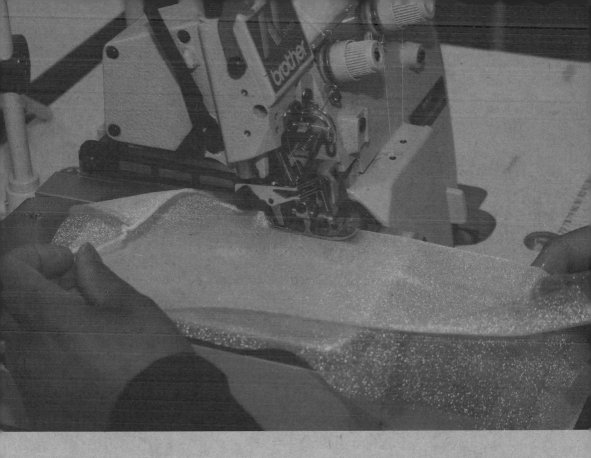

Pongees Ltd
(Silks)
28 Hoxton Square,
London EC1
Tel: 020 7739 9130

Riri Swiss
(Zips and runners)
E.L. Watson 48 Elm Grove
Orpington Kent BR6 0AD
Tel: 01689 836471

R.D. Franks Ltd
(Fashion books and magazines)
5 Winsley Street
London W1W 8HG
Tel: 020 7636 1244

Soho Silks
(Fabrics)
24 Berwick Street,
London W1
Tel: 020 7434 3305

Textile Kings
(Fabrics)
81 Berwick Street,
London W1
Tel: 020 7437 7372

The Button Queen
(Buttons, buckles, fastenings)
19 Marylebone Lane, London
Tel: 020 7935 1505

The Cloth House
(Fabrics)
98 Berwick Street,
London W1
Tel: 020 7287 1555

The Dover Book Shop
(Fashion books)
18 Erlham Street,
London WC2H 9LN
Tel: 020 7836 2111

V.M. Mason
(Zips, eyelets, studs, fastenings,
jeans buttons)
49 Lawrence Road,
Tottenham N15 4EJ
Tel: 020 8802 4227

Whaleys Ltd
(Fabrics, samples available)
Harris Court Gt Horton,
Bradford West Yorks BD7 4EQ
Tel: 01274 576718

William Gee
(Haberdashery, trimmings)
520 Kingsland Road,
London E8 4AJ

2000 Tailoring Ltd
(Buttonholes, zips in any length,
canvas, tailoring tools [call first])
51 Lexington Street,
London W1R 3LG
Tel: 020 7439 1633

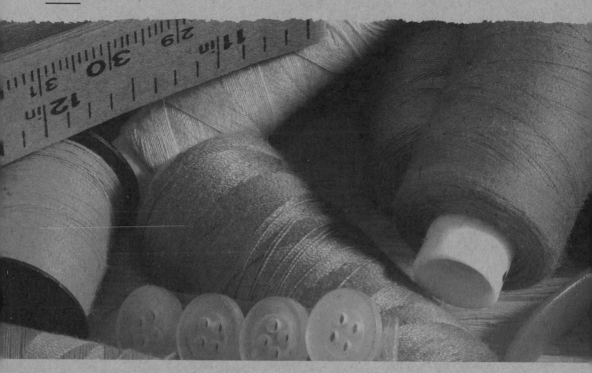

Christian Dior	Donna Karan	Ted Baker
Marios Schwab	Calvin Klein	Paul Smith
Givenchy	Prada	Dolce & Gabbana
Elsa Schiaparelli	Alexander McQueen	Hugo Boss
Peter Pilotto and Christopher De Vos	Christian Lacroix	Joseph
Julien Macdonald	Boudicca	Karin Gardkvist
Versace	Christophe Josse	David Bradley
Meadhamkirchhoff.	Yves Saint Laurent	Hanna Jordan
Jean Paul Gaultier	Unobilie	Gary Kaye
YUKI	Puccini	Robert James Curry and Kimino Homma
Peter Jensen	Vivienne Westwood	

Construction

Felt for chest piece & inside of jacket (covers horse hair)

Horse hair for chest piece & inside of jacket (under felt)

Tim Williams

Helen Manley

Courtney McWilliams

Edina Ozary

Chloe Belle Rees

Laurel Robinson

Valentina Elizabeth

Anette Fischer

Acknowledgements and picture credits

This book is a team effort. A big 'thank you' to everyone who shared their knowledge, talent and time with me: the students of University College for the Creative Arts at Epsom and the students of Middlesex University; the technical team of the fashion department in Epsom, in particular Moira Owusu and Valentina Elizabeth; the fashion team at Epsom who had to put up with my work while I was writing this book and especially John Maclachlan for his encouragement and advice on tailoring.

I was very lucky to have had the help of Peter Close who proofread for me. He was always ready to help at a moment's notice and Peter, I am truly grateful for your advice and help, thank you. This book makes a lot more sense due to the technical drawings of Hannah Jordan, who is a true professional and always in good spirit. Many thanks to you for sharing your talent and time with me. A huge thank you to Gary Kaye, who supplied the illustrations. His work is perfect for my book and delightful to look at. I am glad I had the cheek to ask him to do some work for me; he is a star. Most images have been taken by the talented photographer James Stevens. Thank you for your patience and good humour. It was a pleasure working with you.

'Vielen Dank' Elena Logara-Panteli, you are a busy woman and still you offered your help, thank you for being there for me. Richard Sorger, you got me into this in the first place, thank you for believing in me. I would also like to thank the directors of Robert Ashworth Clothing for Men and Women in Reigate, Surrey; Elizabeth Long and Richard Clews for letting me use their collection for a photo shoot.

A big thank you to Martin Edwards, Robert James Curry, Tim Williams, Marios Schwab, Gemma Ainsworth, Linda Gorbeck, Peter Pilotto, Helen Manley, Clover Stones, Courtney McWilliams, Edina Ozary, Laurel Robinson, Chloe Belle Rees, Karin Gardkvist, Andrew Baker, Adrien Perry Roberts, Calum Mackenzie, Robert Nicolaas de Niet, Vincenza Galati, Sifer Design and the team at AVA Publishing, including Rachel Netherwood, Leafy Robinson and Brian Morris.

Apologies to my family and friends who had to do without me for some time!

Liebe Mama und Papa, danke dass Ihr mich bei meinem Treiben immer unterstuetzt habt. Ohne euch waere das alles nicht moeglich gawesen. Ich hab euch lieb.

My lovely Andrew you are simply my rock and you make great cups of tea, I love you lots.

Picture credits

Cover image courtesy of Rebekah Train; p 3 courtesy of Catwalking.com; p 6 courtesy of David Bradley; p 10 courtesy of Catwalking.com; p 24 courtesy of Catwalking.com; p 26 courtesy of Karin Gardkvist; p 31 courtesy of Catwalking.com; p 34 courtesy of Catwalking.com; p 37 courtesy of Catwalking.com; p 38 courtesy of Catwalking.com; p 46 courtesy of Courtney McWilliams; p 48 courtesy of Catwalking.com; p 51 courtesy of Catwalking.com; p 56 courtesy of Catwalking.com; p 58 courtesy of Vivienne Westwood; p 60 courtesy of Getty; p 70 courtesy of Clover Stones; p 74 (1–4) courtesy of Andrew Baker; pp 74–75 (5–8) copyright J. Braithwaite & Co. (Sewing Machines Ltd); p 76 courtesy of Martin Edwards; p 78 courtesy of Martin Edwards; p 83 courtesy of Catwalking.com; p 90 courtesy of Julien Macdonald; p 93 courtesy of Catwalking.com; p 94 courtesy of Catwalking.com; pp 96–97 courtesy of Valentina Elizabeth; p 99 courtesy of Julien Macdonald; p 101 courtesy of Courtney McWilliams; p 103 courtesy of Catwalking.com; p 104 courtesy of Julien Macdonald; p 106 courtesy of Yuki; p 108 courtesy of Catwalking.com; p 114 courtesy of Catwalking.com; p 120 courtesy of Catwalking.com; pp 126–127 courtesy of Tim Williams; p 128 courtesy of Catwalking.com; p 129 courtesy of Edina Ozary; pp 132–133 courtesy of Peter Pilotto; pp 134–135 courtesy of Robert James Curry and Kimino Homma; p 136 courtesy of Rex Features; p 142 courtesy of Givenchy; p 145 courtesy of Marios Schwab; p 146 courtesy of V&A Images/Victoria & Albert Museum; p 152 courtesy of Caroline Gilbey; p 156 courtesy of Catwalking.com; p 157 courtesy of Julien Macdonald; p 159 courtesy of Julien Macdonald; p 160 Julien Macdonald; p 161 (4) courtesy of Catwalking.com; p 162 courtesy of Laurel Robinson; p 163 courtesy of Puccini; pp 166–167 courtesy of Robert Ashworth Collection; pp 168–169 courtesy of Robert Ashworth Collection; pp 170–171 courtesy of Robert Ashworth Collection; p 177 courtesy of Edina Ozary; p 182 courtesy of Clover Stones; p 186 courtesy of Clover Stones; p 189 courtesy of Clover Stones; pp 12–13, 14, 16, 18–19, 22, 30, 32–33, 40–41, 42, 45, 46, 49, 52–53, 54–55, 57, 68–69, 72–73, 74–75, 77, 79, 80–81, 82, 85, 86, 87, 88, 89, 92, 100–101, 106–107, 110, 113, 115, 116, 117, 118, 119, 122–123, 124, 125, 129, 130, 131, 140, 141, 142, 143, 147, 150, 151, 152, 153, 154, 155, 161 (3), 166, 167, 168, 169, 170, 171, 172–173, 174, 175, 187, 188 and 191 courtesy of James Stevens; pp 15, 35,115, 138–139, 148–149, 163 illustrations by Gary Kaye; pp 17, 20–21, 23, 27, 28–29, 30, 33, 35, 36–37, 39, 40–41, 42–43, 44–45, 46–47, 48, 50, 52–53, 61, 62–63, 66–67, 79, 80–81, 83, 84–85, 86–87, 88–89, 92–93, 95, 96, 101, 107, 158, 160 technical drawings by Hanna Jordan and Amy Morgan.

BASICS
FASHION DESIGN
Working with ethics

Lynne Elvins
Naomi Goulder

Publisher's note

The subject of ethics is not new, yet its consideration within the applied visual arts is perhaps not as prevalent as it might be. Our aim here is to help a new generation of students, educators and practitioners find a methodology for structuring their thoughts and reflections in this vital area.

AVA Publishing hopes that these **Working with ethics** pages provide a platform for consideration and a flexible method for incorporating ethical concerns in the work of educators, students and professionals. Our approach consists of four parts:

The **introduction** is intended to be an accessible snapshot of the ethical landscape, both in terms of historical development and current dominant themes.

The **framework** positions ethical consideration into four areas and poses questions about the practical implications that might occur. Marking your response to each of these questions on the scale shown will allow your reactions to be further explored by comparison.

The **case study** sets out a real project and then poses some ethical questions for further consideration. This is a focus point for a debate rather than a critical analysis so there are no predetermined right or wrong answers.

A selection of **further reading** for you to consider areas of particular interest in more detail.

Ethical: aware-ness/ reflect-ion/ debate

Working with ethics

Ethics is a complex subject that interlaces the idea of responsibilities to society with a wide range of considerations relevant to the character and happiness of the individual. It concerns virtues of compassion, loyalty and strength, but also of confidence, imagination, humour and optimism. As introduced in ancient Greek philosophy, the fundamental ethical question is *what should I do?* How we might pursue a 'good' life not only raises moral concerns about the effects of our actions on others, but also personal concerns about our own integrity.

In modern times the most important and controversial questions in ethics have been the moral ones. With growing populations and improvements in mobility and communications, it is not surprising that considerations about how to structure our lives together on the planet should come to the forefront. For visual artists and communicators it should be no surprise that these considerations will enter into the creative process.

Some ethical considerations are already enshrined in government laws and regulations or in professional codes of conduct. For example, plagiarism and breaches of confidentiality can be punishable offences. Legislation in various nations makes it unlawful to exclude people with disabilities from accessing information or spaces. The trade of ivory as a material has been banned in many countries. In these cases, a clear line has been drawn under what is unacceptable.

But most ethical matters remain open to debate, among experts and lay-people alike, and in the end we have to make our own choices on the basis of our own guiding principles or values. Is it more ethical to work for a charity than for a commercial company? Is it unethical to create something that others find ugly or offensive?

Specific questions such as these may lead to other questions that are more abstract. For example, is it only effects on humans (and what they care about) that are important, or might effects on the natural world require attention too?

Is promoting ethical consequences justified even when it requires ethical sacrifices along the way? Must there be a single unifying theory of ethics (such as the Utilitarian thesis that the right course of action is always the one that leads to the greatest happiness of the greatest number), or might there always be many different ethical values that pull a person in various directions?

As we enter into ethical debate and engage with these dilemmas on a personal and professional level, we may change our views or change our view of others. The real test though is whether, as we reflect on these matters, we change the way we act as well as the way we think. Socrates, the 'father' of philosophy, proposed that people will naturally do 'good' if they know what is right. But this point might only lead us to yet another question: *how do we know what is right?*

You
What are your ethical beliefs?

Central to everything you do will be your attitude to people and issues around you. For some people their ethics are an active part of the decisions they make everyday as a consumer, a voter or a working professional. Others may think about ethics very little and yet this does not automatically make them unethical. Personal beliefs, lifestyle, politics, nationality, religion, gender, class or education can all influence your ethical viewpoint.

Using the scale, where would you place yourself? What do you take into account to make your decision? Compare results with your friends or colleagues.

Your client
What are your terms?

Working relationships are central to whether ethics can be embedded into a project and your conduct on a day-to-day basis is a demonstration of your professional ethics. The decision with the biggest impact is whom you choose to work with in the first place. Cigarette companies or arms traders are often-cited examples when talking about where a line might be drawn, but rarely are real situations so extreme. At what point might you turn down a project on ethical grounds and how much does the reality of having to earn a living affect your ability to choose?

Using the scale, where would you place a project? How does this compare to your personal ethical level?

01 02 03 04 05 06 07 08 09 10   01 02 03 04 05 06 07 08 09 10

Your specifications
What are the impacts of your materials?

In relatively recent times we are learning that many natural materials are in short supply. At the same time we are increasingly aware that some man-made materials can have harmful, long-term effects on people or the planet. How much do you know about the materials that you use? Do you know where they come from, how far they travel and under what conditions they are obtained? When your creation is no longer needed, will it be easy and safe to recycle? Will it disappear without a trace? Are these considerations the responsibility of you or are they out of your hands?

Using the scale, mark how ethical your material choices are.

Your creation
What is the purpose of your work?

Between you, your colleagues and an agreed brief, what will your creation achieve? What purpose will it have in society and will it make a positive contribution? Should your work result in more than commercial success or industry awards? Might your creation help save lives, educate, protect or inspire? Form and function are two established aspects of judging a creation, but there is little consensus on the obligations of visual artists and communicators toward society, or the role they might have in solving social or environmental problems. If you want recognition for being the creator, how responsible are you for what you create and where might that responsibility end?

Using the scale, mark how ethical the purpose of your work is.

01 02 03 04 05 06 07 08 09 10

01 02 03 04 05 06 07 08 09 10

Working with ethics

One aspect of fashion design that raises an ethical dilemma is the way that clothes production has changed in terms of the speed of delivery of products and the now international chain of suppliers. 'Fast fashion' gives shoppers the latest styles sometimes just weeks after they first appeared on the catwalk, at prices that mean they can wear an outfit once or twice and then replace it. Due to lower labour costs in poorer countries, the vast majority of Western clothes are made in Asia, Africa, South America or Eastern Europe in potentially hostile and sometimes inhumane working conditions. It can be common for one piece of clothing to be made up of components from five or more countries, often thousands of miles apart, before they end up in the high-street store. How much responsibility should a fashion designer have in this situation if manufacture is controlled by retailers and demand is driven by consumers? Even if designers wish to minimise the social impact of fashion, what might they most usefully do?

Traditional Hawaiian feather capes (called *'Ahu'ula*) were made from thousands of tiny bird feathers and were an essential part of aristocratic regalia. Initially they were red (*'Ahu'ula* literally means 'red garment') but yellow feathers, being especially rare, became more highly prized and were introduced to the patterning.

The significance of the patterns, as well as their exact age or place of manufacture is largely unknown, despite great interest in their provenance in more recent times. Hawaii was visited in 1778 by English explorer Captain James Cook and feather capes were amongst the objects taken back to Britain.

The basic patterns are thought to reflect gods or ancestral spirits, family connections and an individual's rank or position in society. The base layer for these garments is a fibre net, with the surface made up of bundles of feathers tied to the net in overlapping rows. Red feathers came from the *'i'iwi* or the *'apapane*. Yellow feathers came from a black bird with yellow tufts under each wing called *'oo'oo*, or a *mamo* with yellow feathers above and below the tail.

AIGA
Design Business and Ethics
2007, AIGA

Eaton, Marcia Muelder
Aesthetics and the Good Life
1989, Associated University Press

Ellison, David
Ethics and Aesthetics in European Modernist Literature:
From the Sublime to the Uncanny
2001, Cambridge University Press

Fenner, David E W (Ed)
Ethics and the Arts:
An Anthology
1995, Garland Reference Library of Social Science

Gini, Al and Marcoux, Alexei M
Case Studies in Business Ethics
2005, Prentice Hall

McDonough, William and Braungart, Michael
Cradle to Cradle:
Remaking the Way We Make Things
2002, North Point Press

Papanek, Victor
Design for the Real World:
Making to Measure
1972, Thames and Hudson

United Nations Global Compact
The Ten Principles
www.unglobalcompact.org/AboutTheGC/TheTenPrinciples/index.html

Thousands of feathers were used to make a single cape for a high chief (the feather cape of King Kamehameha the Great is said to have been made from the feathers of around 80,000 birds). Only the highest-ranking chiefs had the resources to acquire enough feathers for a full-length cape, whereas most chiefs wore shorter ones which came to the elbow.

The demand for these feathers was so great that they acquired commercial value and provided a full-time job for professional feather-hunters. These fowlers studied the birds and caught them with nets or with bird lime smeared on branches. As both the *'i'iwi* and *'apapane* were covered with red feathers, the birds were killed and skinned. Other birds were captured at the beginning of the moulting season, when the yellow display feathers were loose and easily removed without damaging the birds.

The royal family of Hawaii eventually abandoned the feather cape as the regalia of rank in favour of military and naval uniforms decorated with braid and gold. The *'oo'oo* and the *mamo* became extinct through the destruction of their forest feeding grounds and imported bird diseases. Silver and gold replaced red and yellow feathers as traded currency and the manufacture of feather capes became a largely forgotten art.

Is it more ethical to create clothing for the masses rather than for a few high-ranking individuals?

Is it unethical to kill animals to make garments?

Would you design and make a feather cape?

Fashion is a form of ugliness so intolerable that we have to alter it every six months.

Oscar Wilde

Working with ethics